# THE LAST TEMPLAR

## THE FALCON TEMPLE

ORIGINAL SCRIPT
## RAYMOND KHOURY

ARTWORK
## MIGUEL LALOR

COLOURS
## THORN

9th CINEBOOK
The 9th Art Publisher

PREVIOUSLY...

After his Templar brothers all perish as the *Falcon Temple* is shipwrecked on the Turkish coast, Martin manages to hide Aimard's coded letter to the masters of the Paris Temple. Shortly afterwards, he is captured, enslaved, and forced to work in a mine in Tuscany...

In the present day, centuries later, at the bottom of a lake in a lost Turkish valley, Reilly and Tess find Aimard's astrolabe – the key to locating the wrecked Templar ship. But Tess abandons Reilly to leave with Vance, fearing that Reilly will not expose the Templars' secret. Or worse: that he will pass it on to the Vatican, who would do anything to keep it hidden for ever...

Original title: Le Dernier Templier – Le Faucon du Temple
Original edition: © Dargaud, 2013 by Khoury & Lalor
www.dargaud.com
All rights reserved
Re-adaptation into English and additional translation: © 2015 Cinebook Ltd
Translator: Mark Bence
Lettering and text layout: Design Amorandi
Printed in Spain by EGEDSA
This edition first published in Great Britain in 2017 by
Cinebook Ltd
56 Beech Avenue
Canterbury, Kent
CT4 7TA
www.cinebook.com
A CIP catalogue record for this book
is available from the British Library
ISBN 978-1-84918-322-2

9th CINEBOOK
The 9th Art Publisher

CARRARA, TUSCANY...

AUGUST 1313...

TWENTY-TWO YEARS AFTER THE SHIPWRECK OF THE *FALCON TEMPLE*...

I AM HERE... STILL HERE...

ALIVE... BARELY. TWO DECADES OF THIS HELL, OR HAS IT BEEN MORE? I CANNOT RECALL... I'VE LOST COUNT OF THE YEARS... ALL I KNOW IS THAT I MUST SURVIVE... I MUST NEVER LOSE HOPE OF ESCAPE...

I OWE IT TO MY ORDER...

CRACK!

???

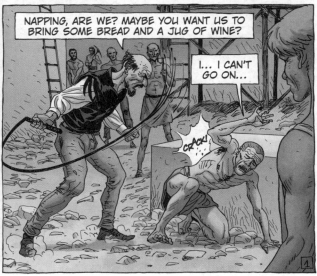

NAPPING, ARE WE? MAYBE YOU WANT US TO BRING SOME BREAD AND A JUG OF WINE?

I... I CAN'T GO ON...

CRACK!

3

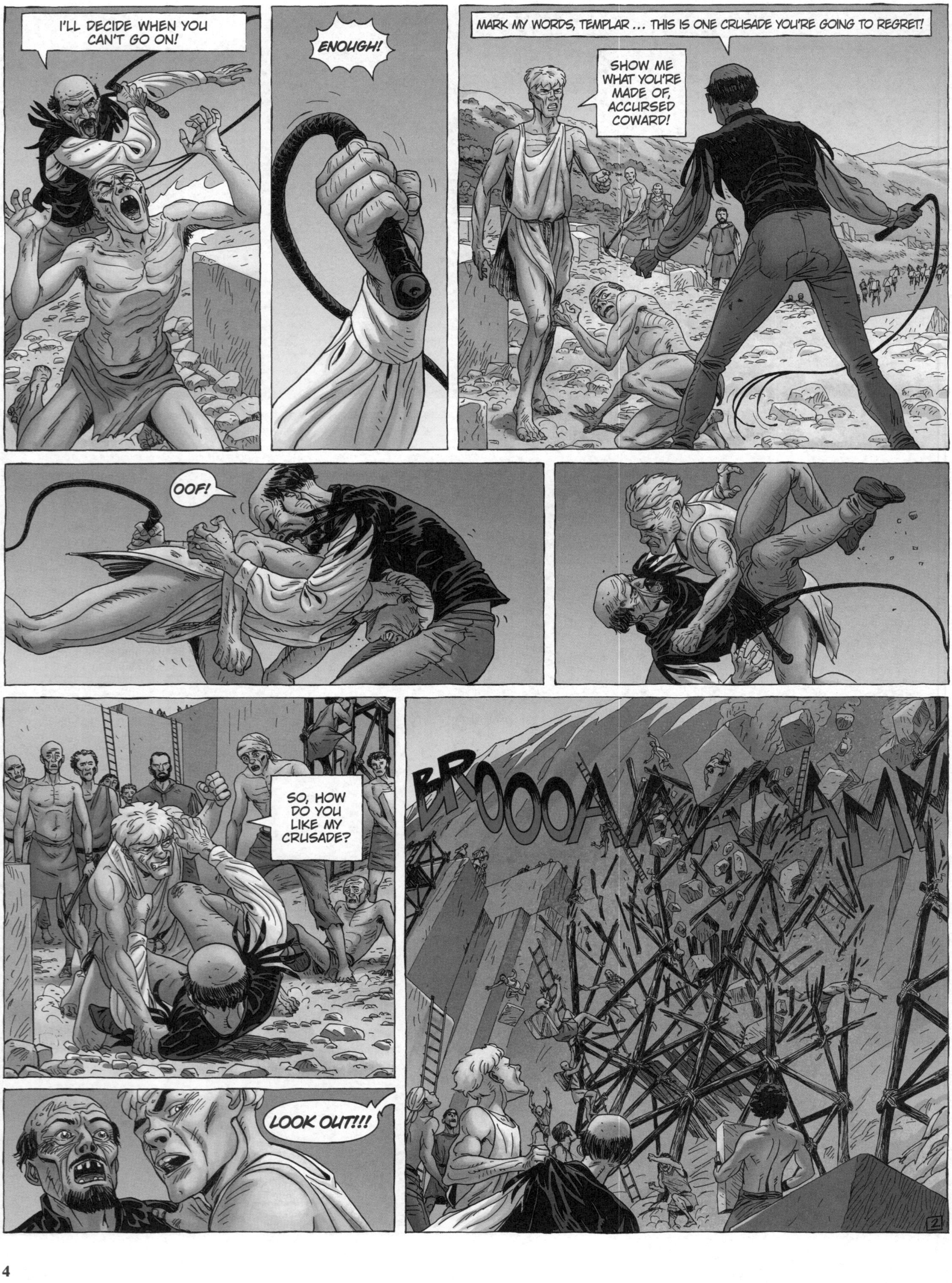
I'LL DECIDE WHEN YOU CAN'T GO ON!
ENOUGH!
MARK MY WORDS, TEMPLAR ... THIS IS ONE CRUSADE YOU'RE GOING TO REGRET!
SHOW ME WHAT YOU'RE MADE OF, ACCURSED COWARD!
OOF!
SO, HOW DO YOU LIKE MY CRUSADE?
LOOK OUT!!!
BROOOA
2

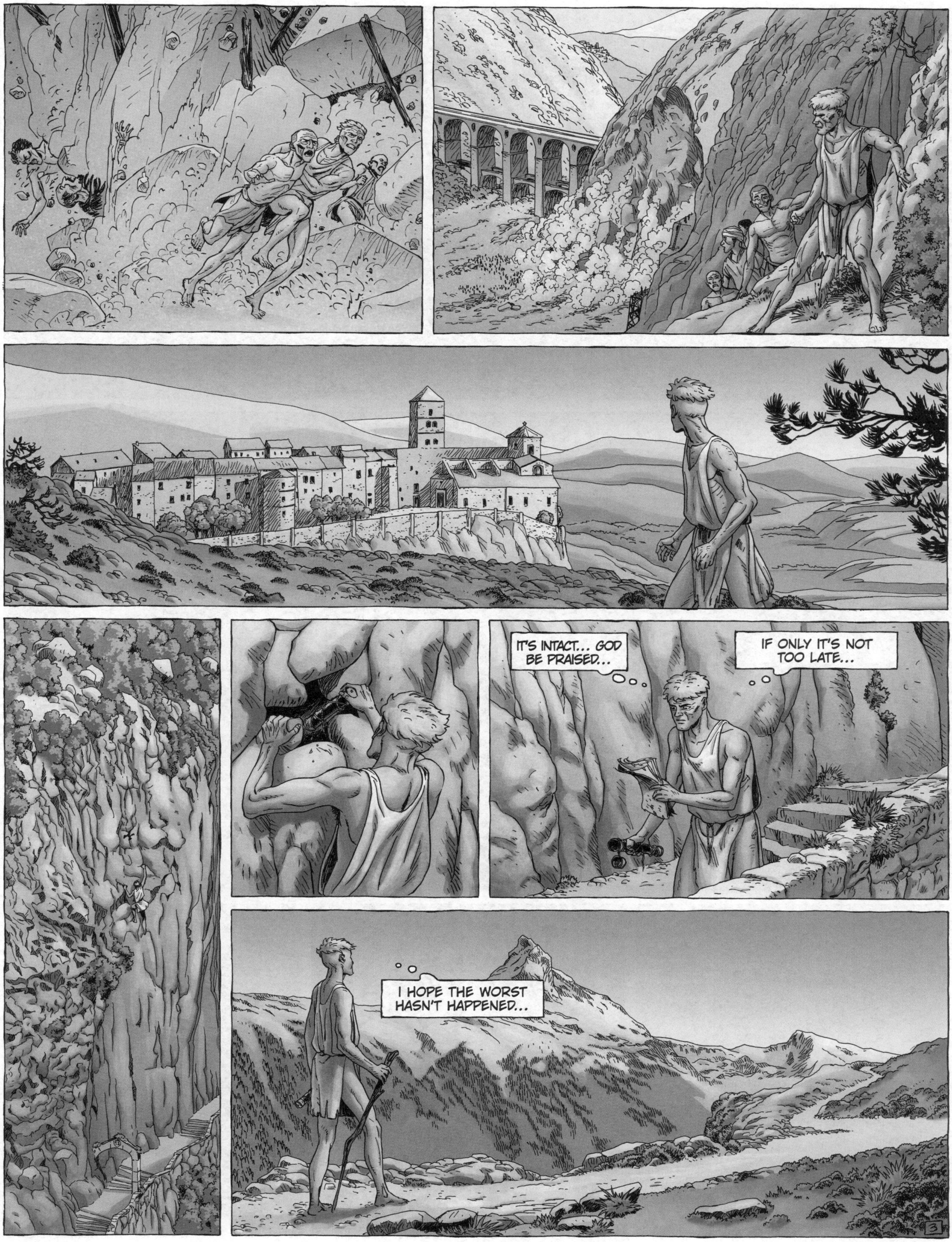
IT'S INTACT... GOD BE PRAISED...
IF ONLY IT'S NOT TOO LATE...
I HOPE THE WORST HASN'T HAPPENED...
3

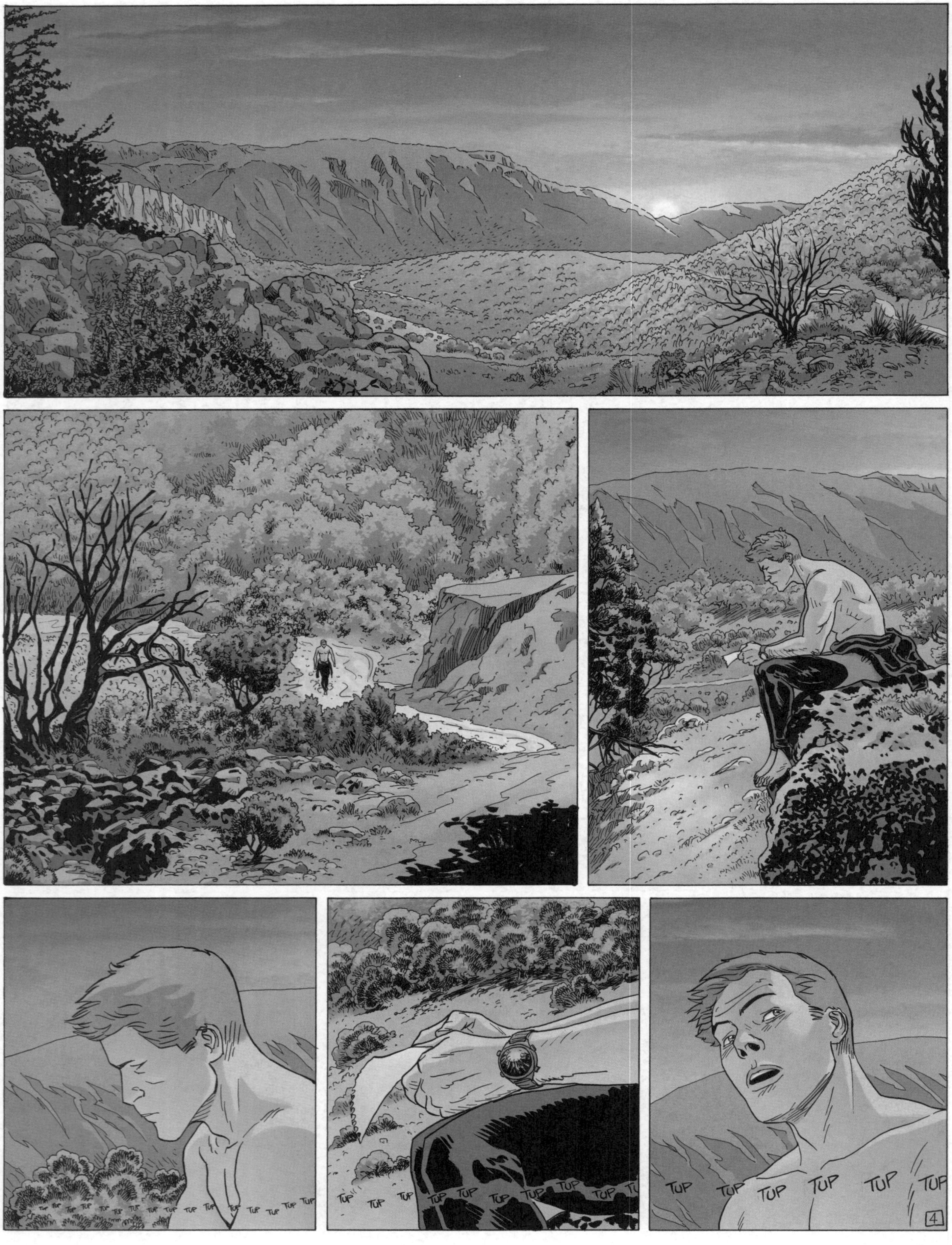
TUP TUP TUP TUP TUP TUP TUP TUP TUP
TUP TUP TUP TUP TUP TUP TUP TUP TUP
TUP TUP TUP TUP TUP TUP
4

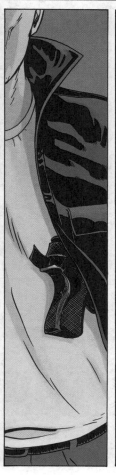

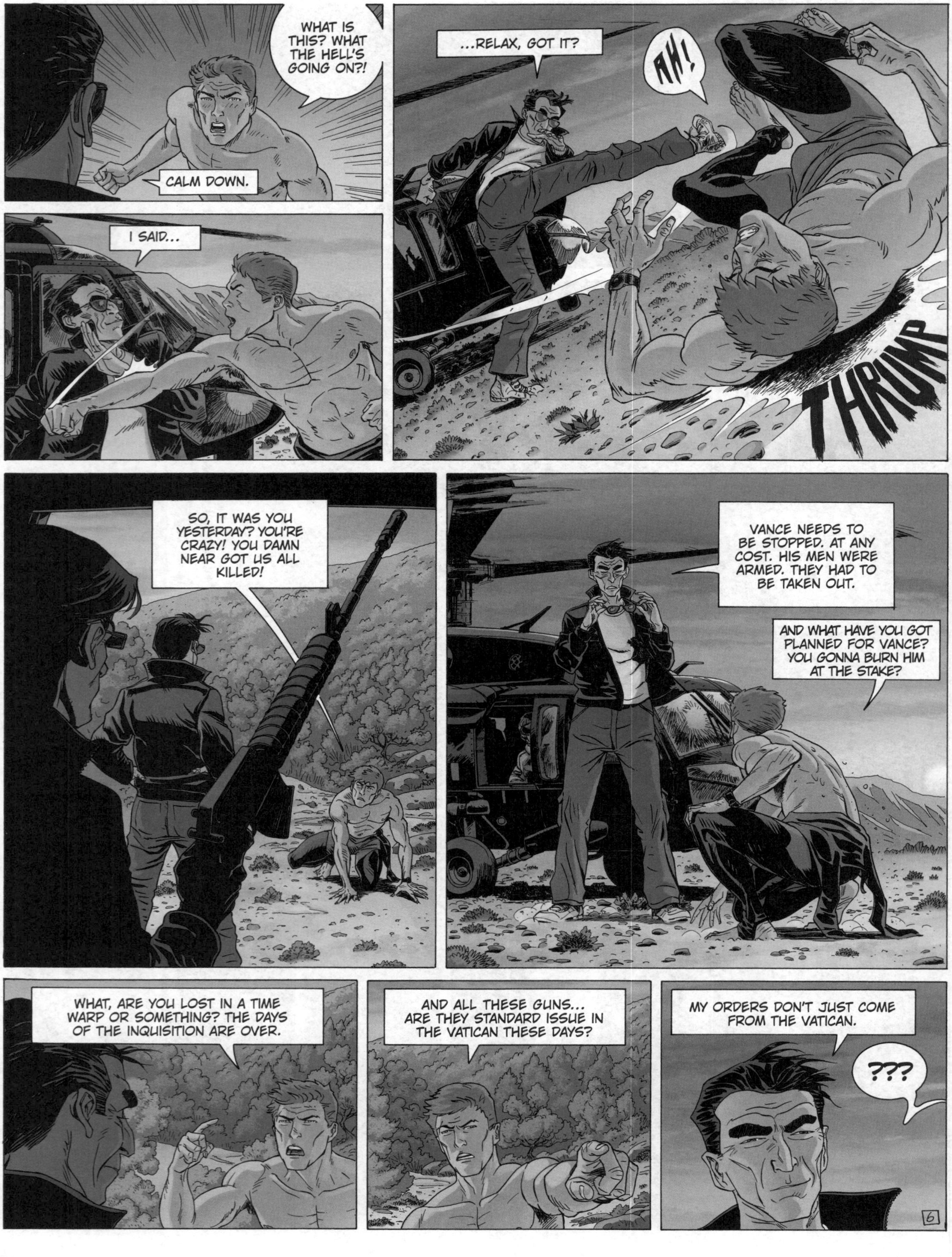
WHAT IS THIS? WHAT THE HELL'S GOING ON?!
CALM DOWN.
I SAID...
...RELAX, GOT IT?
AH!
THRUMP
SO, IT WAS YOU YESTERDAY? YOU'RE CRAZY! YOU DAMN NEAR GOT US ALL KILLED!
VANCE NEEDS TO BE STOPPED. AT ANY COST. HIS MEN WERE ARMED. THEY HAD TO BE TAKEN OUT.
AND WHAT HAVE YOU GOT PLANNED FOR VANCE? YOU GONNA BURN HIM AT THE STAKE?
WHAT, ARE YOU LOST IN A TIME WARP OR SOMETHING? THE DAYS OF THE INQUISITION ARE OVER.
AND ALL THESE GUNS... ARE THEY STANDARD ISSUE IN THE VATICAN THESE DAYS?
MY ORDERS DON'T JUST COME FROM THE VATICAN.
???
6

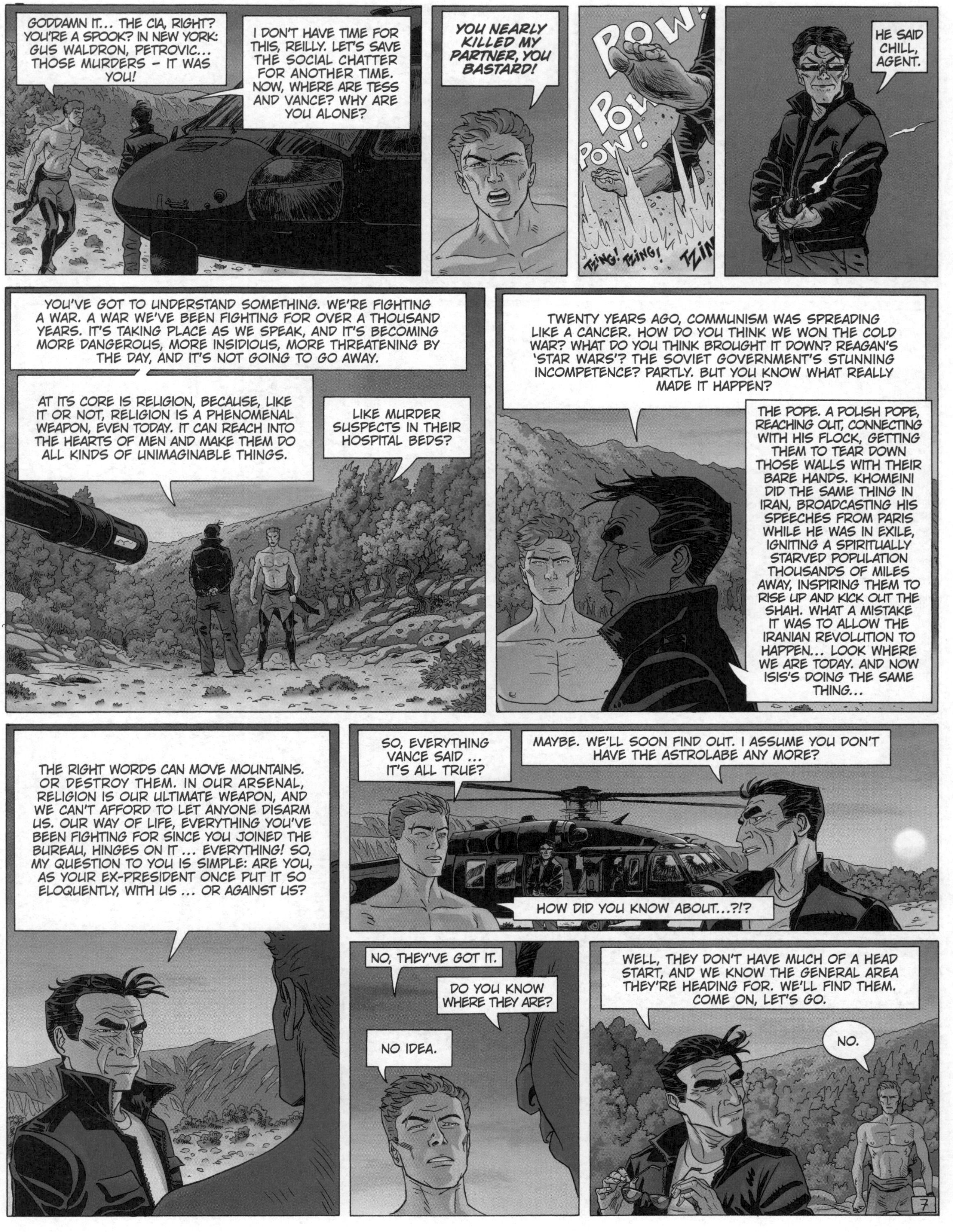

GODDAMN IT... THE CIA, RIGHT? YOU'RE A SPOOK? IN NEW YORK: GUS WALDRON, PETROVIC... THOSE MURDERS – IT WAS YOU!
I DON'T HAVE TIME FOR THIS, REILLY. LET'S SAVE THE SOCIAL CHATTER FOR ANOTHER TIME. NOW, WHERE ARE TESS AND VANCE? WHY ARE YOU ALONE?
YOU NEARLY KILLED MY PARTNER, YOU BASTARD!
POW! POW! POW!
TZING! TZING! TZIN
HE SAID CHILL, AGENT.
YOU'VE GOT TO UNDERSTAND SOMETHING. WE'RE FIGHTING A WAR. A WAR WE'VE BEEN FIGHTING FOR OVER A THOUSAND YEARS. IT'S TAKING PLACE AS WE SPEAK, AND IT'S BECOMING MORE DANGEROUS, MORE INSIDIOUS, MORE THREATENING BY THE DAY, AND IT'S NOT GOING TO GO AWAY.
AT ITS CORE IS RELIGION, BECAUSE, LIKE IT OR NOT, RELIGION IS A PHENOMENAL WEAPON, EVEN TODAY. IT CAN REACH INTO THE HEARTS OF MEN AND MAKE THEM DO ALL KINDS OF UNIMAGINABLE THINGS.
LIKE MURDER SUSPECTS IN THEIR HOSPITAL BEDS?
TWENTY YEARS AGO, COMMUNISM WAS SPREADING LIKE A CANCER. HOW DO YOU THINK WE WON THE COLD WAR? WHAT DO YOU THINK BROUGHT IT DOWN? REAGAN'S 'STAR WARS'? THE SOVIET GOVERNMENT'S STUNNING INCOMPETENCE? PARTLY. BUT YOU KNOW WHAT REALLY MADE IT HAPPEN?
THE POPE. A POLISH POPE, REACHING OUT, CONNECTING WITH HIS FLOCK, GETTING THEM TO TEAR DOWN THOSE WALLS WITH THEIR BARE HANDS. KHOMEINI DID THE SAME THING IN IRAN, BROADCASTING HIS SPEECHES FROM PARIS WHILE HE WAS IN EXILE, IGNITING A SPIRITUALLY STARVED POPULATION THOUSANDS OF MILES AWAY, INSPIRING THEM TO RISE UP AND KICK OUT THE SHAH. WHAT A MISTAKE IT WAS TO ALLOW THE IRANIAN REVOLUTION TO HAPPEN... LOOK WHERE WE ARE TODAY. AND NOW ISIS'S DOING THE SAME THING...
THE RIGHT WORDS CAN MOVE MOUNTAINS. OR DESTROY THEM. IN OUR ARSENAL, RELIGION IS OUR ULTIMATE WEAPON, AND WE CAN'T AFFORD TO LET ANYONE DISARM US. OUR WAY OF LIFE, EVERYTHING YOU'VE BEEN FIGHTING FOR SINCE YOU JOINED THE BUREAU, HINGES ON IT ... EVERYTHING! SO, MY QUESTION TO YOU IS SIMPLE: ARE YOU, AS YOUR EX-PRESIDENT ONCE PUT IT SO ELOQUENTLY, WITH US ... OR AGAINST US?
SO, EVERYTHING VANCE SAID ... IT'S ALL TRUE?
MAYBE. WE'LL SOON FIND OUT. I ASSUME YOU DON'T HAVE THE ASTROLABE ANY MORE?
HOW DID YOU KNOW ABOUT...?!?
NO, THEY'VE GOT IT.
DO YOU KNOW WHERE THEY ARE?
NO IDEA.
WELL, THEY DON'T HAVE MUCH OF A HEAD START, AND WE KNOW THE GENERAL AREA THEY'RE HEADING FOR. WE'LL FIND THEM. COME ON, LET'S GO.
NO.
7

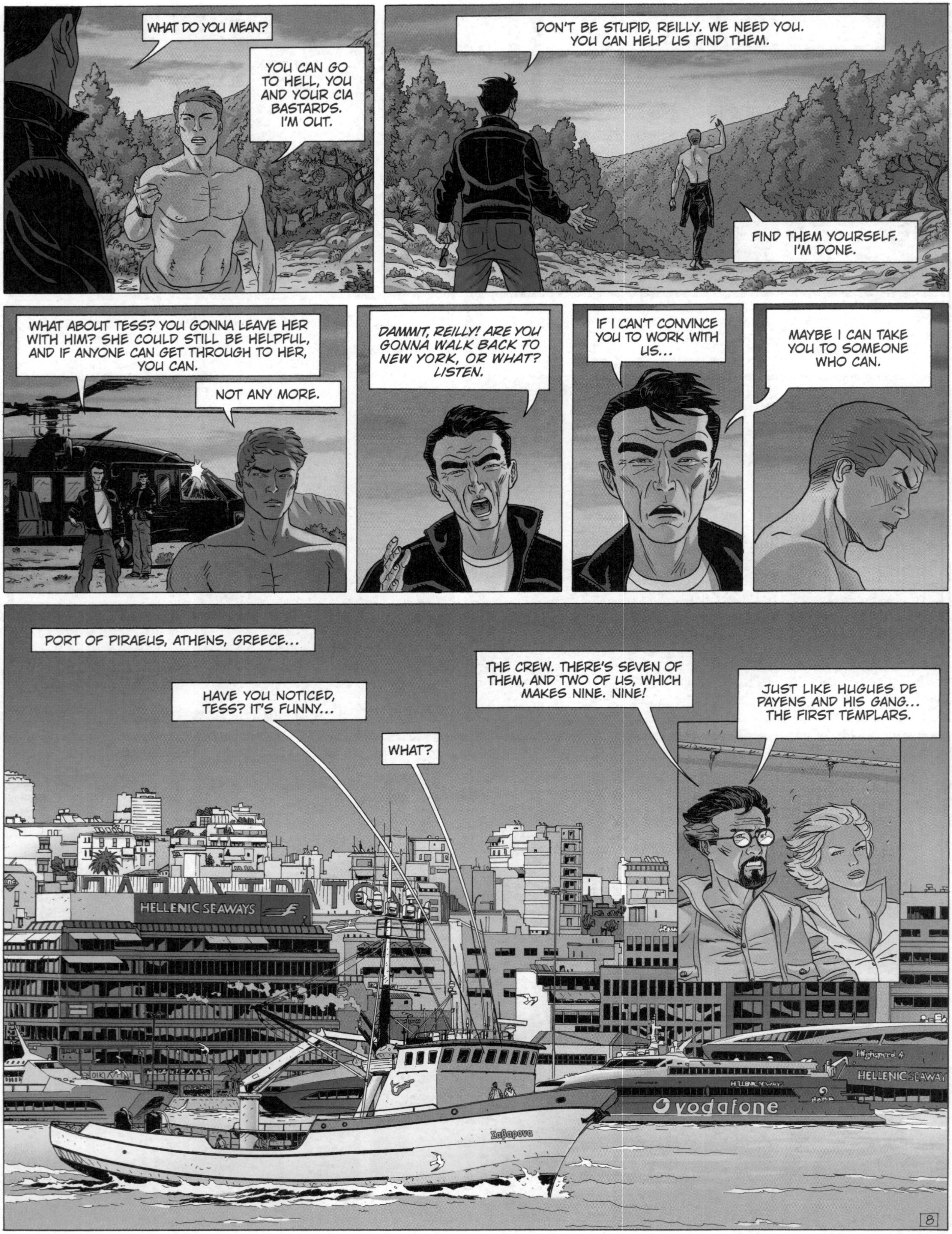
WHAT DO YOU MEAN?
YOU CAN GO TO HELL, YOU AND YOUR CIA BASTARDS. I'M OUT.
DON'T BE STUPID, REILLY. WE NEED YOU. YOU CAN HELP US FIND THEM.
FIND THEM YOURSELF. I'M DONE.
WHAT ABOUT TESS? YOU GONNA LEAVE HER WITH HIM? SHE COULD STILL BE HELPFUL, AND IF ANYONE CAN GET THROUGH TO HER, YOU CAN.
NOT ANY MORE.
DAMMIT, REILLY! ARE YOU GONNA WALK BACK TO NEW YORK, OR WHAT? LISTEN.
IF I CAN'T CONVINCE YOU TO WORK WITH US...
MAYBE I CAN TAKE YOU TO SOMEONE WHO CAN.
PORT OF PIRAEUS, ATHENS, GREECE...
HELLENIC SEAWAYS
HAVE YOU NOTICED, TESS? IT'S FUNNY...
WHAT?
THE CREW. THERE'S SEVEN OF THEM, AND TWO OF US, WHICH MAKES NINE. NINE!
JUST LIKE HUGUES DE PAYENS AND HIS GANG... THE FIRST TEMPLARS.
HELLENIC SEAWAYS
vodafone
8

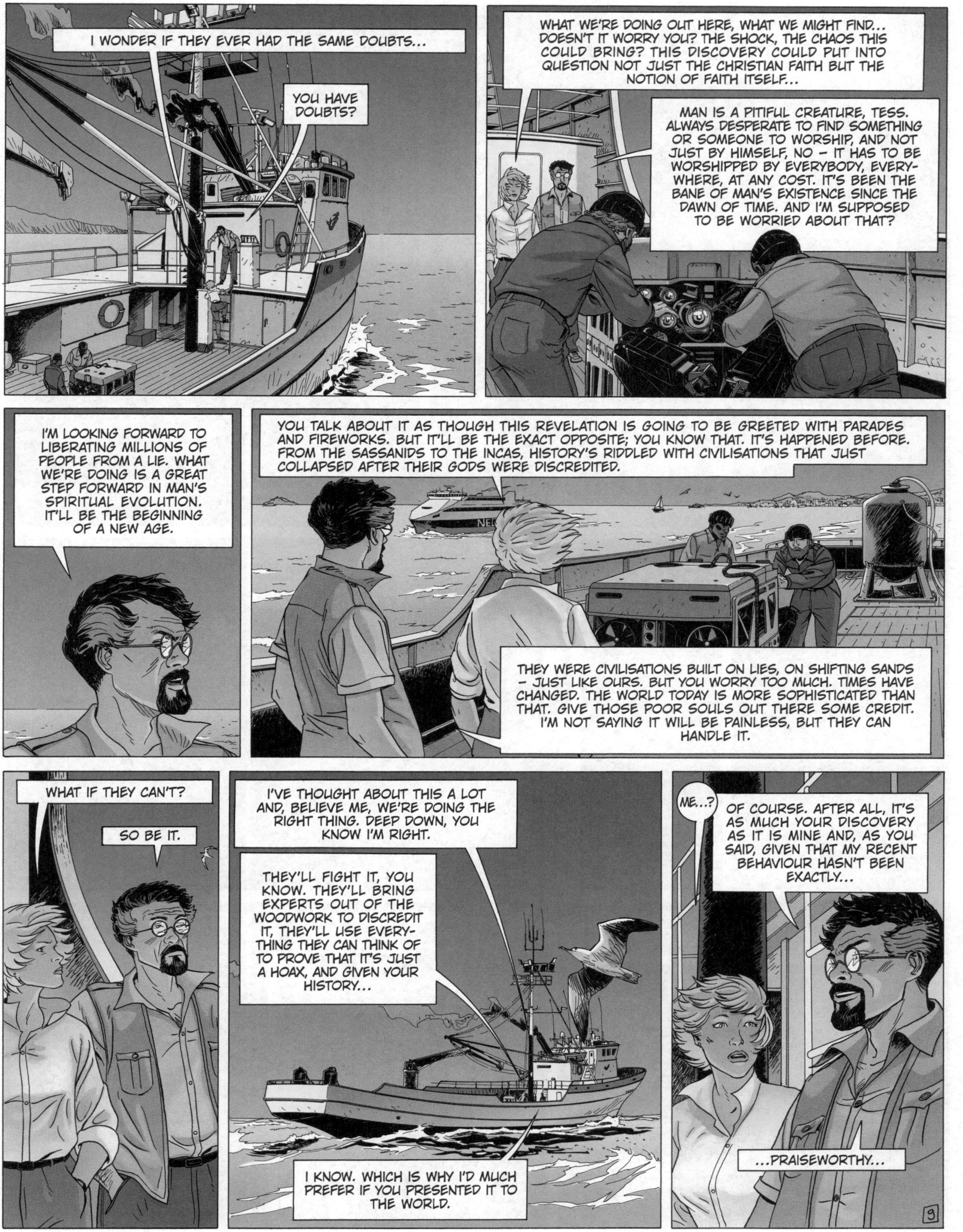

I WONDER IF THEY EVER HAD THE SAME DOUBTS...
YOU HAVE DOUBTS?
WHAT WE'RE DOING OUT HERE, WHAT WE MIGHT FIND... DOESN'T IT WORRY YOU? THE SHOCK, THE CHAOS THIS COULD BRING? THIS DISCOVERY COULD PUT INTO QUESTION NOT JUST THE CHRISTIAN FAITH BUT THE NOTION OF FAITH ITSELF...
MAN IS A PITIFUL CREATURE, TESS. ALWAYS DESPERATE TO FIND SOMETHING OR SOMEONE TO WORSHIP, AND NOT JUST BY HIMSELF, NO – IT HAS TO BE WORSHIPPED BY EVERYBODY, EVERY-WHERE, AT ANY COST. IT'S BEEN THE BANE OF MAN'S EXISTENCE SINCE THE DAWN OF TIME. AND I'M SUPPOSED TO BE WORRIED ABOUT THAT?
I'M LOOKING FORWARD TO LIBERATING MILLIONS OF PEOPLE FROM A LIE. WHAT WE'RE DOING IS A GREAT STEP FORWARD IN MAN'S SPIRITUAL EVOLUTION. IT'LL BE THE BEGINNING OF A NEW AGE.
YOU TALK ABOUT IT AS THOUGH THIS REVELATION IS GOING TO BE GREETED WITH PARADES AND FIREWORKS. BUT IT'LL BE THE EXACT OPPOSITE; YOU KNOW THAT. IT'S HAPPENED BEFORE. FROM THE SASSANIDS TO THE INCAS, HISTORY'S RIDDLED WITH CIVILISATIONS THAT JUST COLLAPSED AFTER THEIR GODS WERE DISCREDITED.
THEY WERE CIVILISATIONS BUILT ON LIES, ON SHIFTING SANDS – JUST LIKE OURS. BUT YOU WORRY TOO MUCH. TIMES HAVE CHANGED. THE WORLD TODAY IS MORE SOPHISTICATED THAN THAT. GIVE THOSE POOR SOULS OUT THERE SOME CREDIT. I'M NOT SAYING IT WILL BE PAINLESS, BUT THEY CAN HANDLE IT.
WHAT IF THEY CAN'T?
SO BE IT.
I'VE THOUGHT ABOUT THIS A LOT AND, BELIEVE ME, WE'RE DOING THE RIGHT THING. DEEP DOWN, YOU KNOW I'M RIGHT.
THEY'LL FIGHT IT, YOU KNOW. THEY'LL BRING EXPERTS OUT OF THE WOODWORK TO DISCREDIT IT, THEY'LL USE EVERY-THING THEY CAN THINK OF TO PROVE THAT IT'S JUST A HOAX, AND GIVEN YOUR HISTORY...
I KNOW. WHICH IS WHY I'D MUCH PREFER IF YOU PRESENTED IT TO THE WORLD.
ME...?
OF COURSE. AFTER ALL, IT'S AS MUCH YOUR DISCOVERY AS IT IS MINE AND, AS YOU SAID, GIVEN THAT MY RECENT BEHAVIOUR HASN'T BEEN EXACTLY...
...PRAISEWORTHY...
9

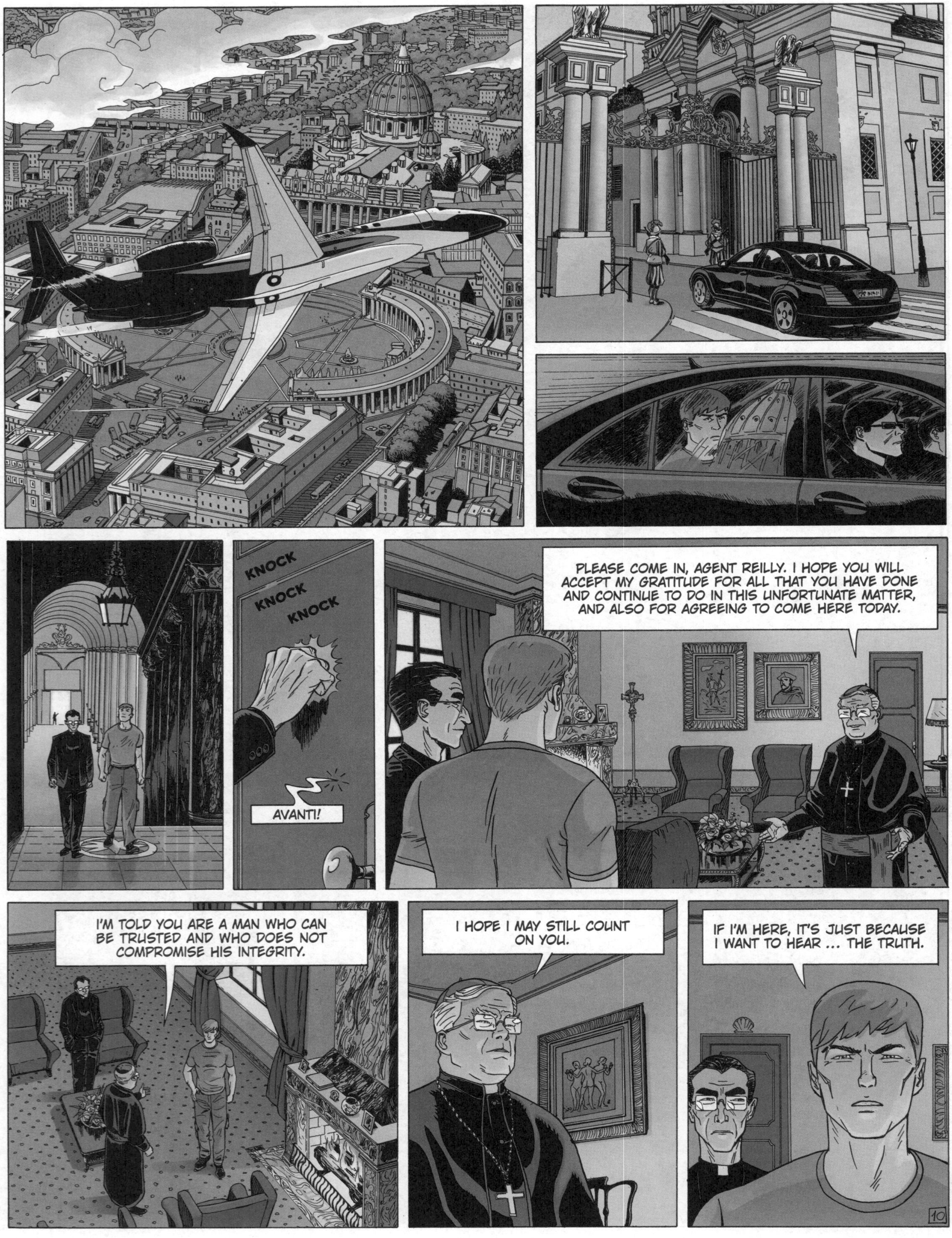
KNOCK
KNOCK
KNOCK
AVANTI!
PLEASE COME IN, AGENT REILLY. I HOPE YOU WILL ACCEPT MY GRATITUDE FOR ALL THAT YOU HAVE DONE AND CONTINUE TO DO IN THIS UNFORTUNATE MATTER, AND ALSO FOR AGREEING TO COME HERE TODAY.
I'M TOLD YOU ARE A MAN WHO CAN BE TRUSTED AND WHO DOES NOT COMPROMISE HIS INTEGRITY.
I HOPE I MAY STILL COUNT ON YOU.
IF I'M HERE, IT'S JUST BECAUSE I WANT TO HEAR ... THE TRUTH.
10

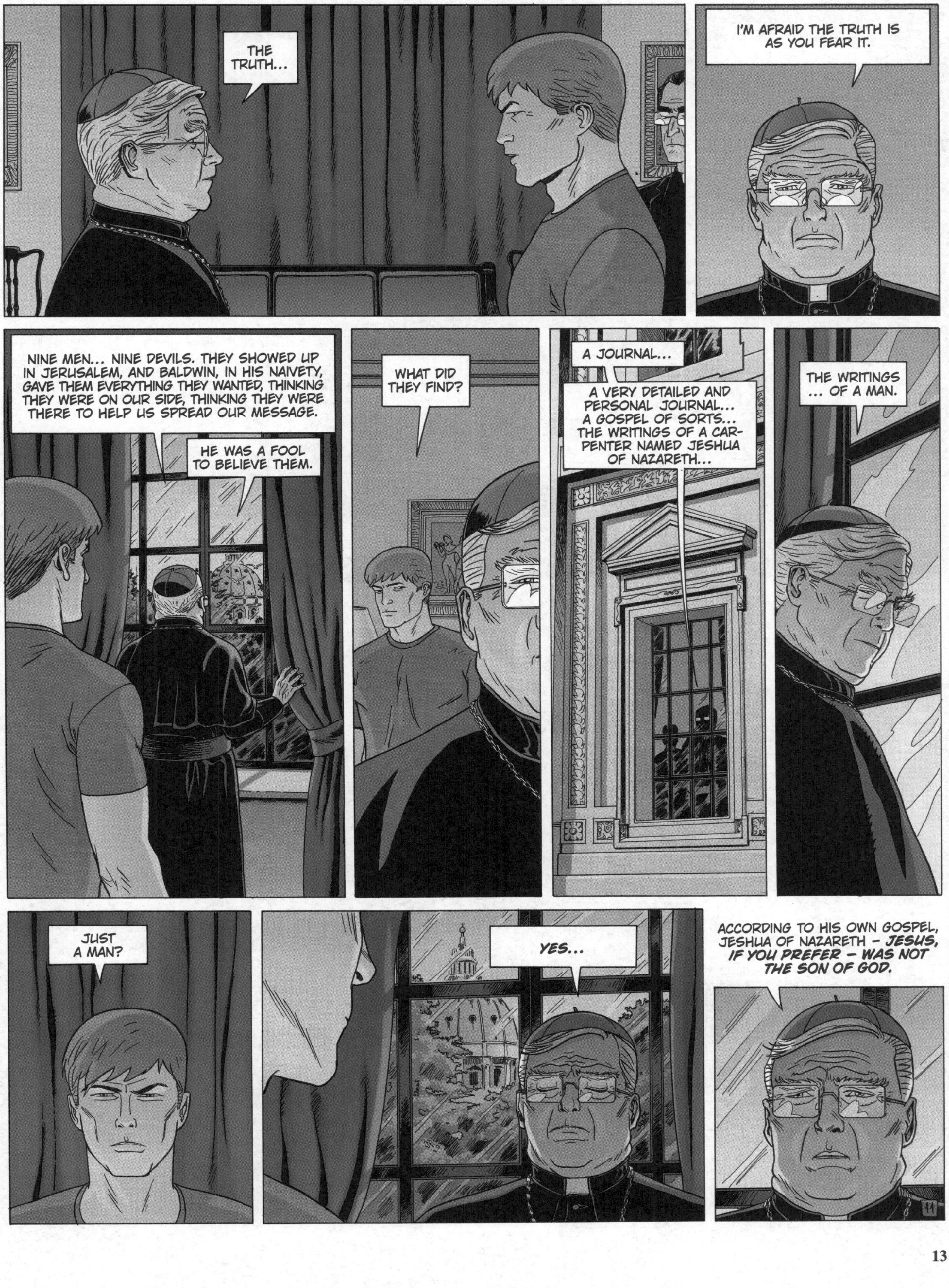
THE TRUTH...
I'M AFRAID THE TRUTH IS AS YOU FEAR IT.
NINE MEN... NINE DEVILS. THEY SHOWED UP IN JERUSALEM, AND BALDWIN, IN HIS NAIVETY, GAVE THEM EVERYTHING THEY WANTED, THINKING THEY WERE ON OUR SIDE, THINKING THEY WERE THERE TO HELP US SPREAD OUR MESSAGE.
HE WAS A FOOL TO BELIEVE THEM.
WHAT DID THEY FIND?
A JOURNAL...
A VERY DETAILED AND PERSONAL JOURNAL... A GOSPEL OF SORTS... THE WRITINGS OF A CAR-PENTER NAMED JESHUA OF NAZARETH...
THE WRITINGS ... OF A MAN.
JUST A MAN?
YES...
ACCORDING TO HIS OWN GOSPEL, JESHUA OF NAZARETH – JESUS, IF YOU PREFER – WAS NOT THE SON OF GOD.
11

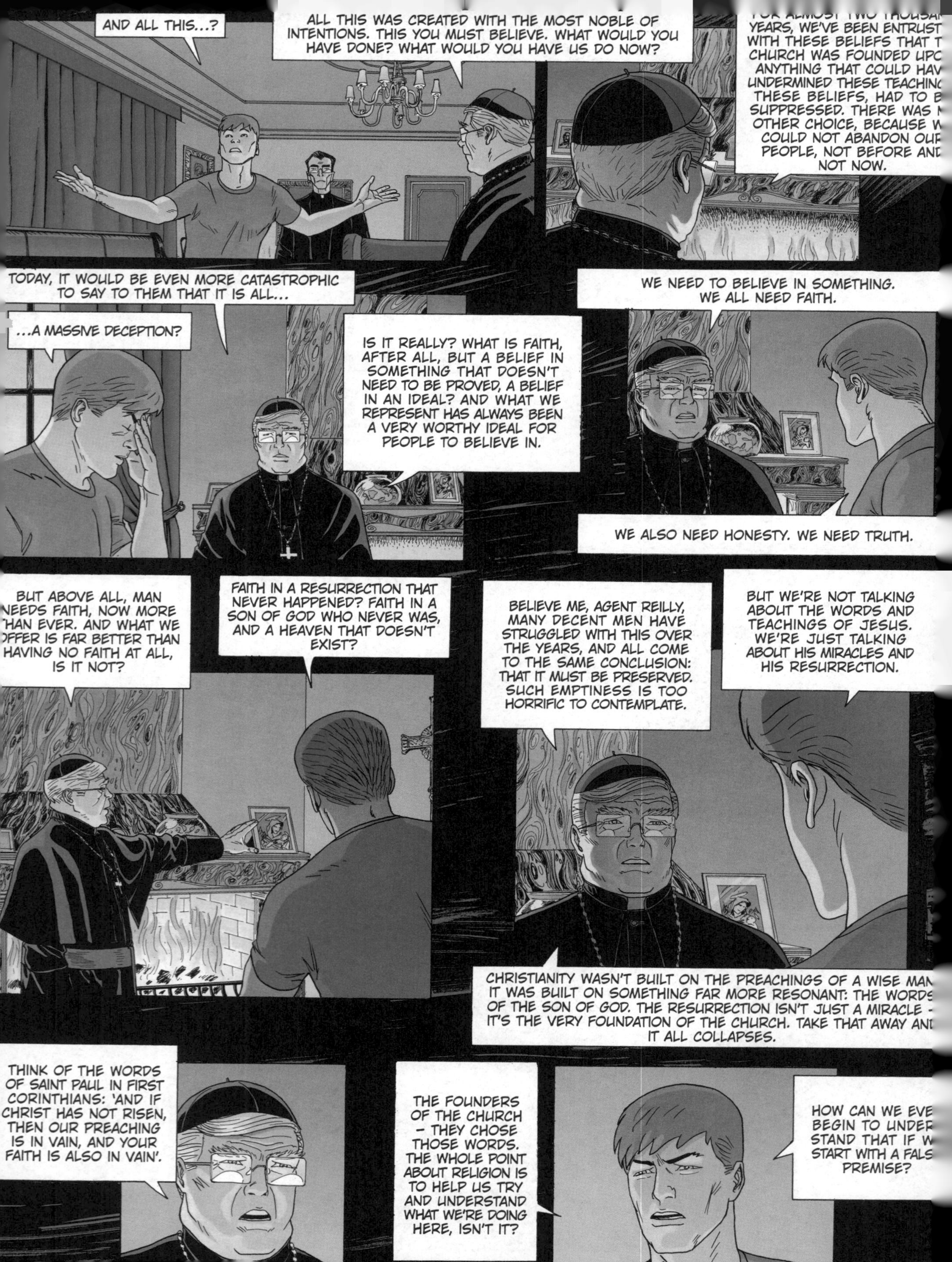
AND ALL THIS...?
ALL THIS WAS CREATED WITH THE MOST NOBLE OF INTENTIONS. THIS YOU MUST BELIEVE. WHAT WOULD YOU HAVE DONE? WHAT WOULD YOU HAVE US DO NOW?
YEARS, WE'VE BEEN ENTRUST WITH THESE BELIEFS THAT T CHURCH WAS FOUNDED UPO ANYTHING THAT COULD HAV UNDERMINED THESE TEACHING THESE BELIEFS, HAD TO B SUPPRESSED. THERE WAS N OTHER CHOICE, BECAUSE W COULD NOT ABANDON OUR PEOPLE, NOT BEFORE AND NOT NOW.
TODAY, IT WOULD BE EVEN MORE CATASTROPHIC TO SAY TO THEM THAT IT IS ALL...
...A MASSIVE DECEPTION?
IS IT REALLY? WHAT IS FAITH, AFTER ALL, BUT A BELIEF IN SOMETHING THAT DOESN'T NEED TO BE PROVED, A BELIEF IN AN IDEAL? AND WHAT WE REPRESENT HAS ALWAYS BEEN A VERY WORTHY IDEAL FOR PEOPLE TO BELIEVE IN.
WE NEED TO BELIEVE IN SOMETHING. WE ALL NEED FAITH.
WE ALSO NEED HONESTY. WE NEED TRUTH.
BUT ABOVE ALL, MAN NEEDS FAITH, NOW MORE THAN EVER. AND WHAT WE OFFER IS FAR BETTER THAN HAVING NO FAITH AT ALL, IS IT NOT?
FAITH IN A RESURRECTION THAT NEVER HAPPENED? FAITH IN A SON OF GOD WHO NEVER WAS, AND A HEAVEN THAT DOESN'T EXIST?
BELIEVE ME, AGENT REILLY, MANY DECENT MEN HAVE STRUGGLED WITH THIS OVER THE YEARS, AND ALL COME TO THE SAME CONCLUSION: THAT IT MUST BE PRESERVED. SUCH EMPTINESS IS TOO HORRIFIC TO CONTEMPLATE.
BUT WE'RE NOT TALKING ABOUT THE WORDS AND TEACHINGS OF JESUS. WE'RE JUST TALKING ABOUT HIS MIRACLES AND HIS RESURRECTION.
CHRISTIANITY WASN'T BUILT ON THE PREACHINGS OF A WISE MAN IT WAS BUILT ON SOMETHING FAR MORE RESONANT: THE WORDS OF THE SON OF GOD. THE RESURRECTION ISN'T JUST A MIRACLE – IT'S THE VERY FOUNDATION OF THE CHURCH. TAKE THAT AWAY AND IT ALL COLLAPSES.
THINK OF THE WORDS OF SAINT PAUL IN FIRST CORINTHIANS: 'AND IF CHRIST HAS NOT RISEN, THEN OUR PREACHING IS IN VAIN, AND YOUR FAITH IS ALSO IN VAIN'.
THE FOUNDERS OF THE CHURCH – THEY CHOSE THOSE WORDS. THE WHOLE POINT ABOUT RELIGION IS TO HELP US TRY AND UNDERSTAND WHAT WE'RE DOING HERE, ISN'T IT?
HOW CAN WE EVE BEGIN TO UNDER STAND THAT IF W START WITH A FALS PREMISE?

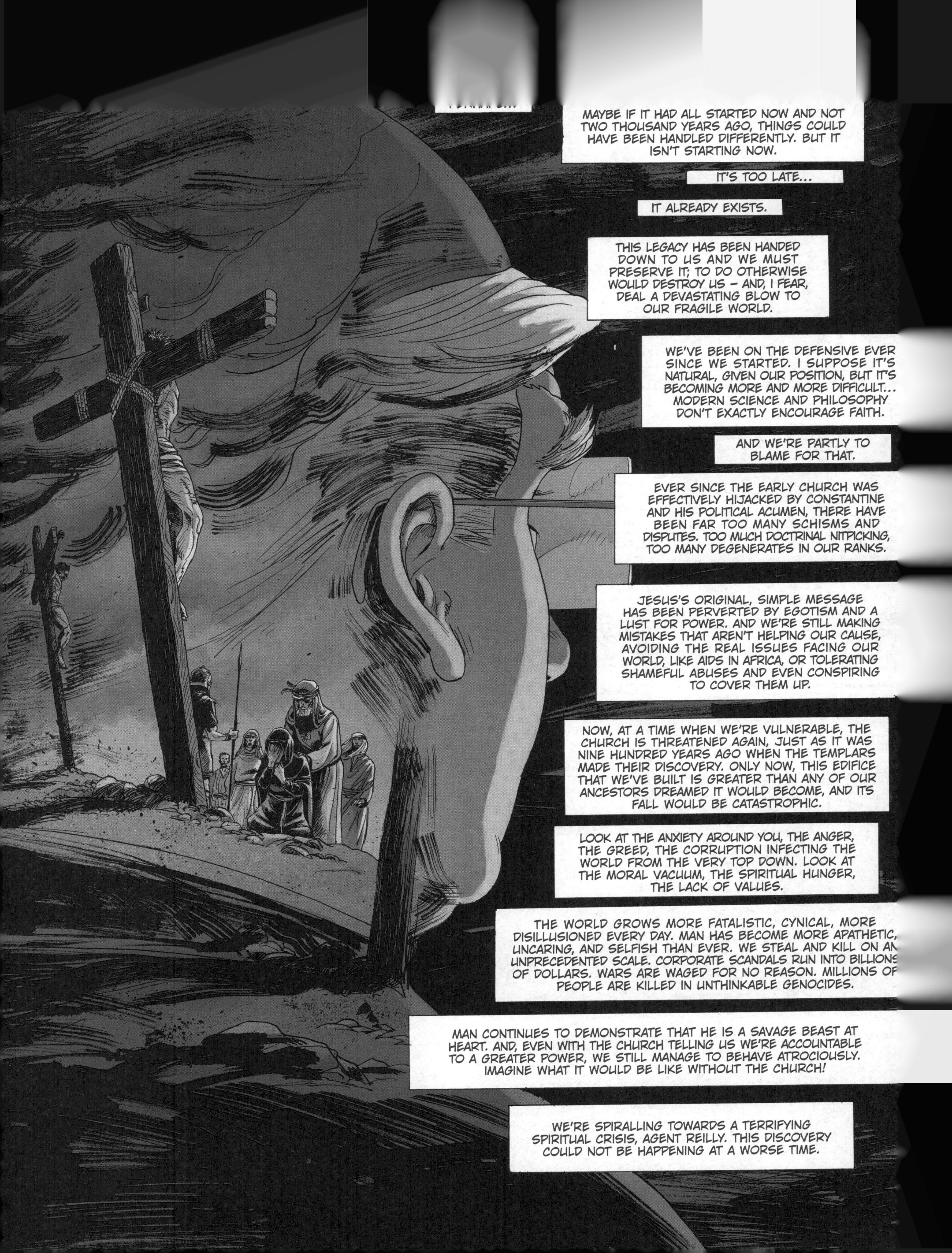
MAYBE IF IT HAD ALL STARTED NOW AND NOT TWO THOUSAND YEARS AGO, THINGS COULD HAVE BEEN HANDLED DIFFERENTLY. BUT IT ISN'T STARTING NOW.
IT'S TOO LATE...
IT ALREADY EXISTS.
THIS LEGACY HAS BEEN HANDED DOWN TO US AND WE MUST PRESERVE IT; TO DO OTHERWISE WOULD DESTROY US – AND, I FEAR, DEAL A DEVASTATING BLOW TO OUR FRAGILE WORLD.
WE'VE BEEN ON THE DEFENSIVE EVER SINCE WE STARTED. I SUPPOSE IT'S NATURAL, GIVEN OUR POSITION, BUT IT'S BECOMING MORE AND MORE DIFFICULT... MODERN SCIENCE AND PHILOSOPHY DON'T EXACTLY ENCOURAGE FAITH.
AND WE'RE PARTLY TO BLAME FOR THAT.
EVER SINCE THE EARLY CHURCH WAS EFFECTIVELY HIJACKED BY CONSTANTINE AND HIS POLITICAL ACUMEN, THERE HAVE BEEN FAR TOO MANY SCHISMS AND DISPUTES. TOO MUCH DOCTRINAL NITPICKING, TOO MANY DEGENERATES IN OUR RANKS.
JESUS'S ORIGINAL, SIMPLE MESSAGE HAS BEEN PERVERTED BY EGOTISM AND A LUST FOR POWER. AND WE'RE STILL MAKING MISTAKES THAT AREN'T HELPING OUR CAUSE, AVOIDING THE REAL ISSUES FACING OUR WORLD, LIKE AIDS IN AFRICA, OR TOLERATING SHAMEFUL ABUSES AND EVEN CONSPIRING TO COVER THEM UP.
NOW, AT A TIME WHEN WE'RE VULNERABLE, THE CHURCH IS THREATENED AGAIN, JUST AS IT WAS NINE HUNDRED YEARS AGO WHEN THE TEMPLARS MADE THEIR DISCOVERY. ONLY NOW, THIS EDIFICE THAT WE'VE BUILT IS GREATER THAN ANY OF OUR ANCESTORS DREAMED IT WOULD BECOME, AND ITS FALL WOULD BE CATASTROPHIC.
LOOK AT THE ANXIETY AROUND YOU, THE ANGER, THE GREED, THE CORRUPTION INFECTING THE WORLD FROM THE VERY TOP DOWN. LOOK AT THE MORAL VACUUM, THE SPIRITUAL HUNGER, THE LACK OF VALUES.
THE WORLD GROWS MORE FATALISTIC, CYNICAL, MORE DISILLUSIONED EVERY DAY. MAN HAS BECOME MORE APATHETIC, UNCARING, AND SELFISH THAN EVER. WE STEAL AND KILL ON AN UNPRECEDENTED SCALE. CORPORATE SCANDALS RUN INTO BILLIONS OF DOLLARS. WARS ARE WAGED FOR NO REASON. MILLIONS OF PEOPLE ARE KILLED IN UNTHINKABLE GENOCIDES.
MAN CONTINUES TO DEMONSTRATE THAT HE IS A SAVAGE BEAST AT HEART. AND, EVEN WITH THE CHURCH TELLING US WE'RE ACCOUNTABLE TO A GREATER POWER, WE STILL MANAGE TO BEHAVE ATROCIOUSLY. IMAGINE WHAT IT WOULD BE LIKE WITHOUT THE CHURCH!
WE'RE SPIRALLING TOWARDS A TERRIFYING SPIRITUAL CRISIS, AGENT REILLY. THIS DISCOVERY COULD NOT BE HAPPENING AT A WORSE TIME.

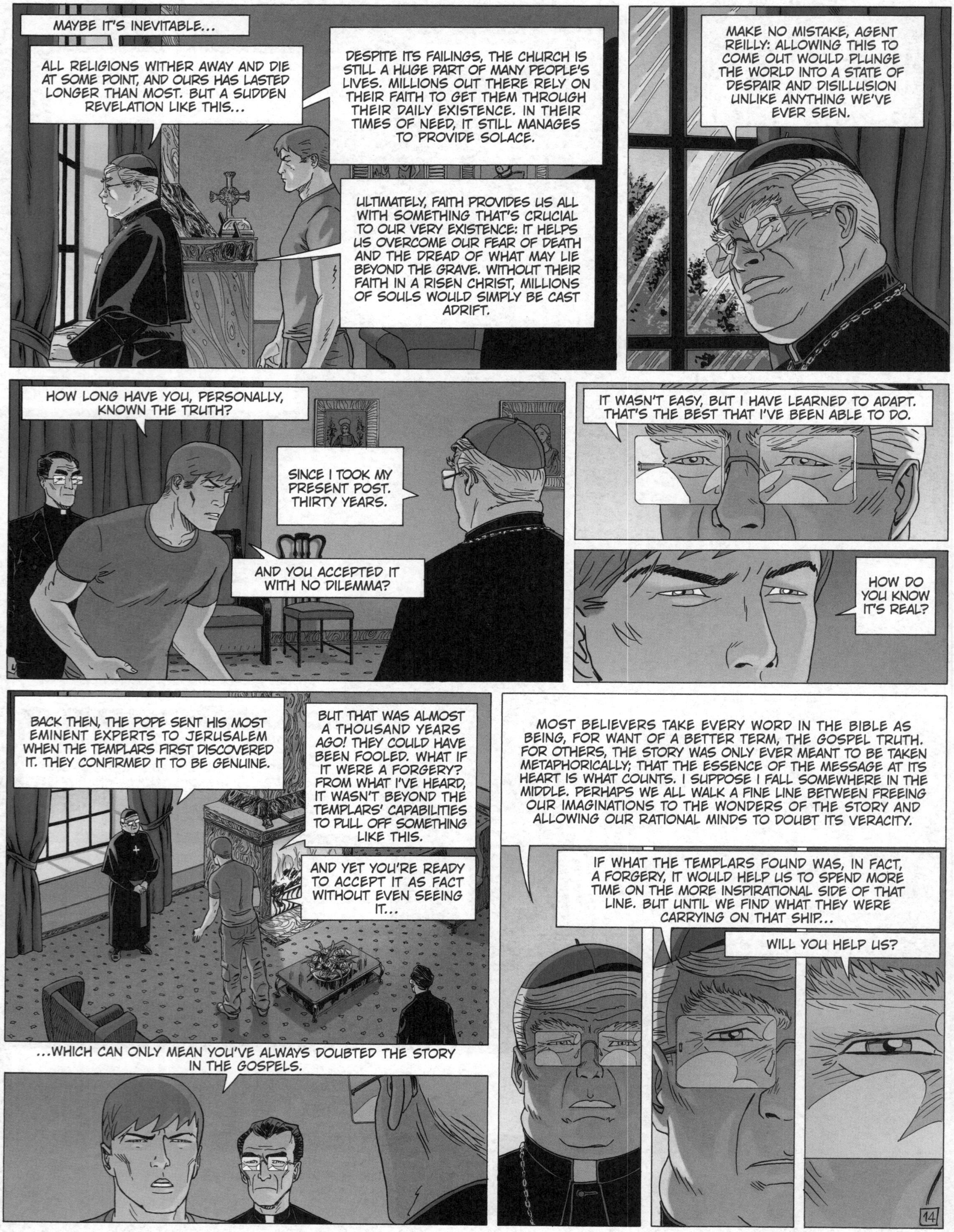
MAYBE IT'S INEVITABLE...
ALL RELIGIONS WITHER AWAY AND DIE AT SOME POINT, AND OURS HAS LASTED LONGER THAN MOST. BUT A SUDDEN REVELATION LIKE THIS...
DESPITE ITS FAILINGS, THE CHURCH IS STILL A HUGE PART OF MANY PEOPLE'S LIVES. MILLIONS OUT THERE RELY ON THEIR FAITH TO GET THEM THROUGH THEIR DAILY EXISTENCE. IN THEIR TIMES OF NEED, IT STILL MANAGES TO PROVIDE SOLACE.
ULTIMATELY, FAITH PROVIDES US ALL WITH SOMETHING THAT'S CRUCIAL TO OUR VERY EXISTENCE: IT HELPS US OVERCOME OUR FEAR OF DEATH AND THE DREAD OF WHAT MAY LIE BEYOND THE GRAVE. WITHOUT THEIR FAITH IN A RISEN CHRIST, MILLIONS OF SOULS WOULD SIMPLY BE CAST ADRIFT.
MAKE NO MISTAKE, AGENT REILLY: ALLOWING THIS TO COME OUT WOULD PLUNGE THE WORLD INTO A STATE OF DESPAIR AND DISILLUSION UNLIKE ANYTHING WE'VE EVER SEEN.
HOW LONG HAVE YOU, PERSONALLY, KNOWN THE TRUTH?
SINCE I TOOK MY PRESENT POST. THIRTY YEARS.
AND YOU ACCEPTED IT WITH NO DILEMMA?
IT WASN'T EASY, BUT I HAVE LEARNED TO ADAPT. THAT'S THE BEST THAT I'VE BEEN ABLE TO DO.
HOW DO YOU KNOW IT'S REAL?
BACK THEN, THE POPE SENT HIS MOST EMINENT EXPERTS TO JERUSALEM WHEN THE TEMPLARS FIRST DISCOVERED IT. THEY CONFIRMED IT TO BE GENUINE.
BUT THAT WAS ALMOST A THOUSAND YEARS AGO! THEY COULD HAVE BEEN FOOLED. WHAT IF IT WERE A FORGERY? FROM WHAT I'VE HEARD, IT WASN'T BEYOND THE TEMPLARS' CAPABILITIES TO PULL OFF SOMETHING LIKE THIS.
AND YET YOU'RE READY TO ACCEPT IT AS FACT WITHOUT EVEN SEEING IT...
...WHICH CAN ONLY MEAN YOU'VE ALWAYS DOUBTED THE STORY IN THE GOSPELS.
MOST BELIEVERS TAKE EVERY WORD IN THE BIBLE AS BEING, FOR WANT OF A BETTER TERM, THE GOSPEL TRUTH. FOR OTHERS, THE STORY WAS ONLY EVER MEANT TO BE TAKEN METAPHORICALLY; THAT THE ESSENCE OF THE MESSAGE AT ITS HEART IS WHAT COUNTS. I SUPPOSE I FALL SOMEWHERE IN THE MIDDLE. PERHAPS WE ALL WALK A FINE LINE BETWEEN FREEING OUR IMAGINATIONS TO THE WONDERS OF THE STORY AND ALLOWING OUR RATIONAL MINDS TO DOUBT ITS VERACITY.
IF WHAT THE TEMPLARS FOUND WAS, IN FACT, A FORGERY, IT WOULD HELP US TO SPEND MORE TIME ON THE MORE INSPIRATIONAL SIDE OF THAT LINE. BUT UNTIL WE FIND WHAT THEY WERE CARRYING ON THAT SHIP...
WILL YOU HELP US?
14

WELL?

NO, IT'S NOT THE *FALCON TEMPLE*. LOOK...

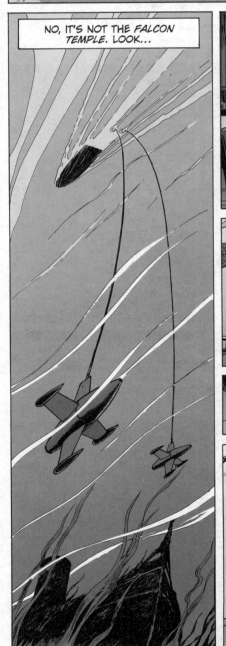

...THERE SHOULD BE, AT MOST, HALF A TON OF IRON LEFT IN THE *FALCON TEMPLE'S* REMAINS. BUT HERE, THE MAGNETO-METER'S SHOWING NEARLY THREE TONS...

ARE YOU SURE?

SORRY, BUT IT'S A MORE RECENT WRECK...

OK, LET'S CARRY ON...

WE MUST HAVE FOUND EVERY WRECK IN THE MEDITERRANEAN SINCE WE GOT HERE...

THE *FALCON* IS HERE SOMEWHERE. I CAN FEEL IT. IT'S JUST A LITTLE HARD TO PINPOINT, THAT'S ALL. BUT WE'LL FIND IT EVENTUALLY. ANOTHER THREE DAYS AND WE'LL HAVE FINISHED TRAWLING THE SEARCH SITE, WON'T WE?

YES, BUT I'M NOT SURE WE'VE GOT THAT LONG.

WHY NOT?

TAKE A LOOK.

BUT ... THE SKY WAS CLEAR THIS MORNING.

I KNOW, AND THE WEATHER RADAR SHOWED NOTHING EITHER. IT'S VERY ODD; I'VE NEVER SEEN A STORM COME OUT OF NOWHERE LIKE THAT...

WE CAN'T STOP. WE'RE CLOSE TO OUR GOAL. I'M SURE WE SHOULD PRESS ON...

WE'LL DO WHAT WE CAN, BUT ... PERHAPS WE WON'T HAVE A CHOICE...

15

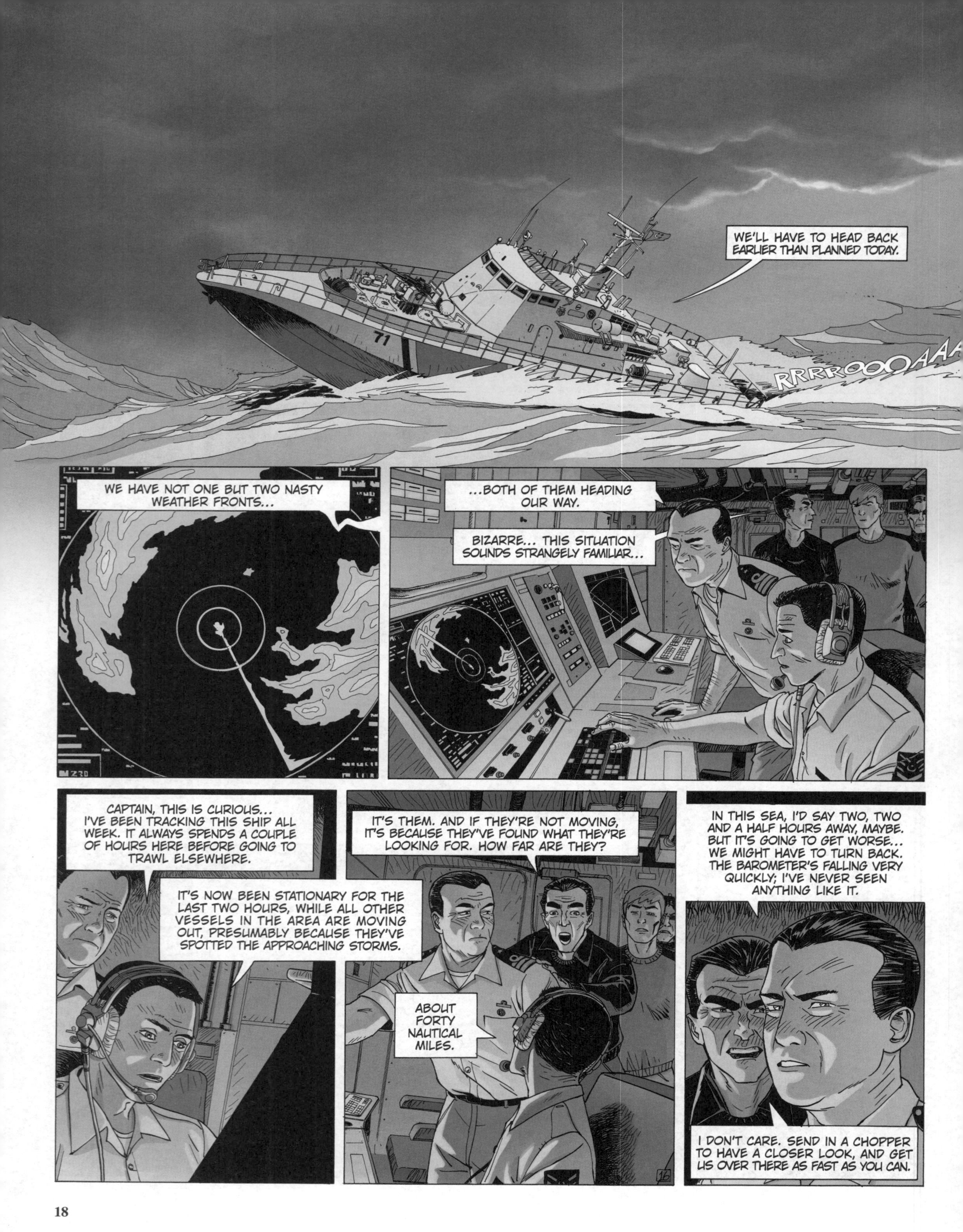

WE'LL HAVE TO HEAD BACK EARLIER THAN PLANNED TODAY.
RRRROOOAAA
WE HAVE NOT ONE BUT TWO NASTY WEATHER FRONTS...
...BOTH OF THEM HEADING OUR WAY.
BIZARRE... THIS SITUATION SOUNDS STRANGELY FAMILIAR...
CAPTAIN, THIS IS CURIOUS... I'VE BEEN TRACKING THIS SHIP ALL WEEK. IT ALWAYS SPENDS A COUPLE OF HOURS HERE BEFORE GOING TO TRAWL ELSEWHERE.
IT'S NOW BEEN STATIONARY FOR THE LAST TWO HOURS, WHILE ALL OTHER VESSELS IN THE AREA ARE MOVING OUT, PRESUMABLY BECAUSE THEY'VE SPOTTED THE APPROACHING STORMS.
IT'S THEM. AND IF THEY'RE NOT MOVING, IT'S BECAUSE THEY'VE FOUND WHAT THEY'RE LOOKING FOR. HOW FAR ARE THEY?
ABOUT FORTY NAUTICAL MILES.
IN THIS SEA, I'D SAY TWO, TWO AND A HALF HOURS AWAY, MAYBE. BUT IT'S GOING TO GET WORSE... WE MIGHT HAVE TO TURN BACK. THE BAROMETER'S FALLING VERY QUICKLY; I'VE NEVER SEEN ANYTHING LIKE IT.
I DON'T CARE. SEND IN A CHOPPER TO HAVE A CLOSER LOOK, AND GET US OVER THERE AS FAST AS YOU CAN.

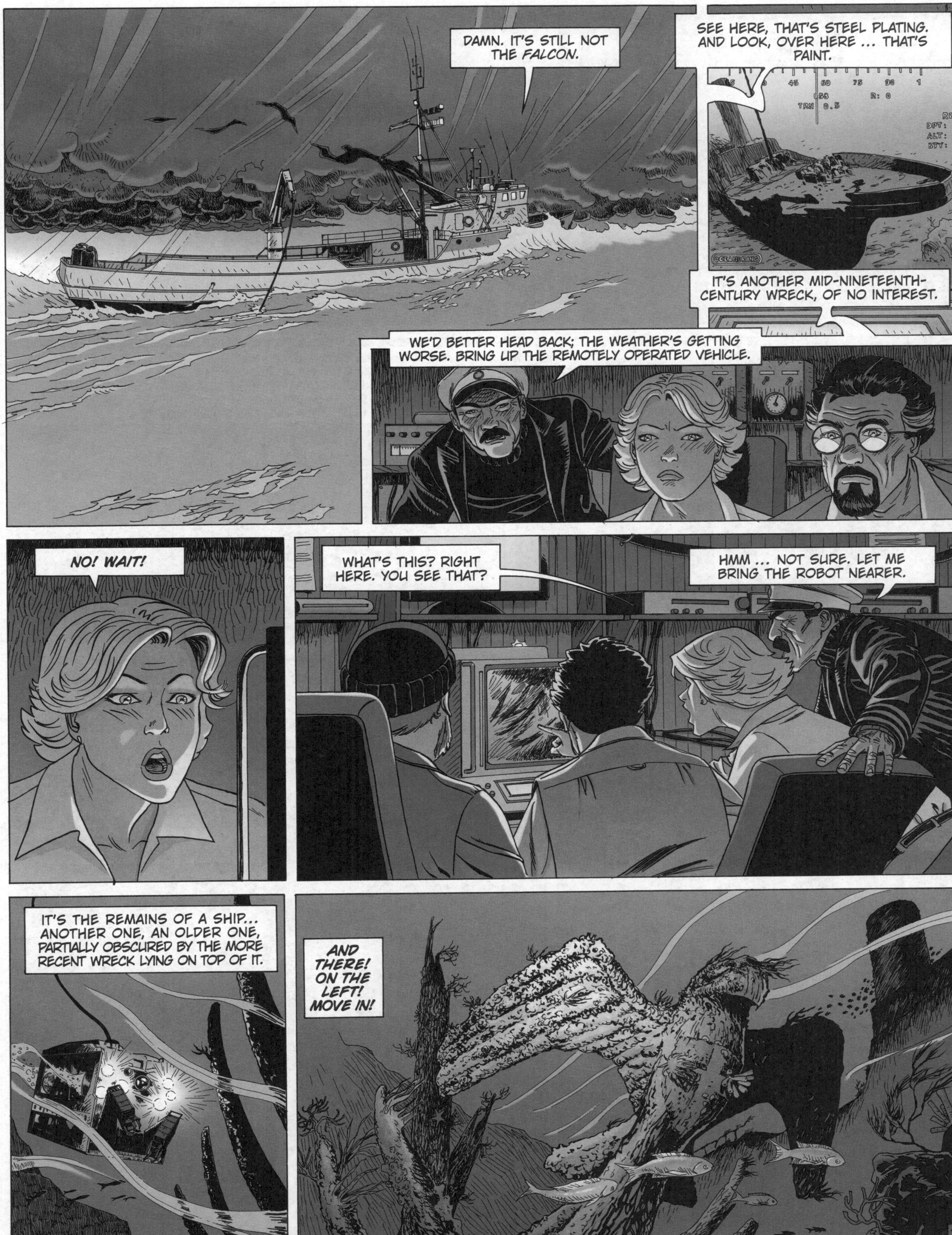

DAMN. IT'S STILL NOT THE *FALCON*.
SEE HERE, THAT'S STEEL PLATING. AND LOOK, OVER HERE ... THAT'S PAINT.
IT'S ANOTHER MID-NINETEENTH-CENTURY WRECK, OF NO INTEREST.
WE'D BETTER HEAD BACK; THE WEATHER'S GETTING WORSE. BRING UP THE REMOTELY OPERATED VEHICLE.
*NO! WAIT!*
WHAT'S THIS? RIGHT HERE. YOU SEE THAT?
HMM ... NOT SURE. LET ME BRING THE ROBOT NEARER.
IT'S THE REMAINS OF A SHIP... ANOTHER ONE, AN OLDER ONE, PARTIALLY OBSCURED BY THE MORE RECENT WRECK LYING ON TOP OF IT.
*AND THERE! ON THE LEFT! MOVE IN!*
17

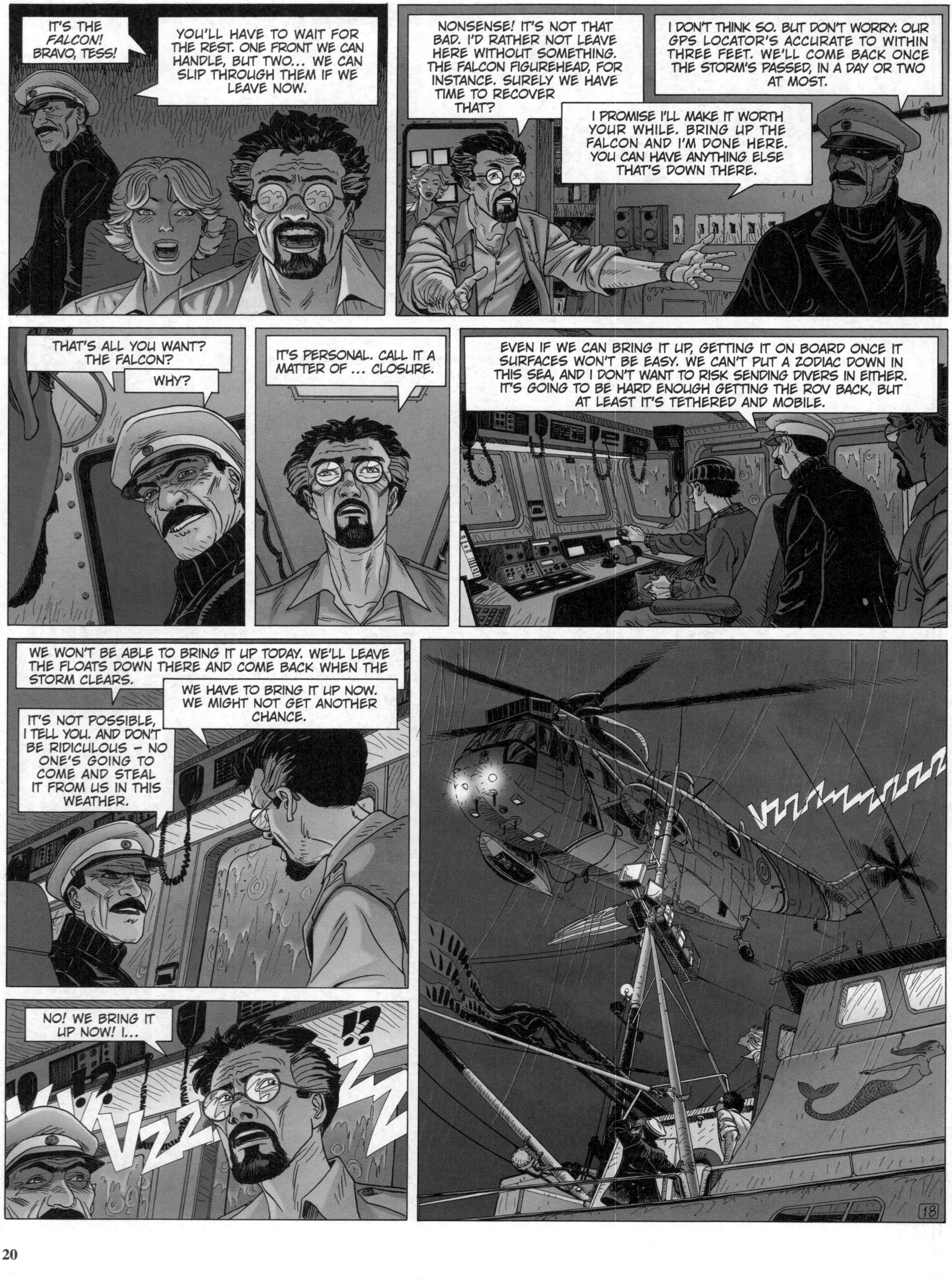
IT'S THE FALCON! BRAVO, TESS!
YOU'LL HAVE TO WAIT FOR THE REST. ONE FRONT WE CAN HANDLE, BUT TWO... WE CAN SLIP THROUGH THEM IF WE LEAVE NOW.
NONSENSE! IT'S NOT THAT BAD. I'D RATHER NOT LEAVE HERE WITHOUT SOMETHING. THE FALCON FIGUREHEAD, FOR INSTANCE. SURELY WE HAVE TIME TO RECOVER THAT?
I DON'T THINK SO. BUT DON'T WORRY: OUR GPS LOCATOR'S ACCURATE TO WITHIN THREE FEET. WE'LL COME BACK ONCE THE STORM'S PASSED, IN A DAY OR TWO AT MOST.
I PROMISE I'LL MAKE IT WORTH YOUR WHILE. BRING UP THE FALCON AND I'M DONE HERE. YOU CAN HAVE ANYTHING ELSE THAT'S DOWN THERE.
THAT'S ALL YOU WANT? THE FALCON?
WHY?
IT'S PERSONAL. CALL IT A MATTER OF ... CLOSURE.
EVEN IF WE CAN BRING IT UP, GETTING IT ON BOARD ONCE IT SURFACES WON'T BE EASY. WE CAN'T PUT A ZODIAC DOWN IN THIS SEA, AND I DON'T WANT TO RISK SENDING DIVERS IN EITHER. IT'S GOING TO BE HARD ENOUGH GETTING THE ROV BACK, BUT AT LEAST IT'S TETHERED AND MOBILE.
WE WON'T BE ABLE TO BRING IT UP TODAY. WE'LL LEAVE THE FLOATS DOWN THERE AND COME BACK WHEN THE STORM CLEARS.
WE HAVE TO BRING IT UP NOW. WE MIGHT NOT GET ANOTHER CHANCE.
IT'S NOT POSSIBLE, I TELL YOU. AND DON'T BE RIDICULOUS – NO ONE'S GOING TO COME AND STEAL IT FROM US IN THIS WEATHER.
NO! WE BRING IT UP NOW! I...
!?
!?
VZZZ
VZZZZZZZZ
18

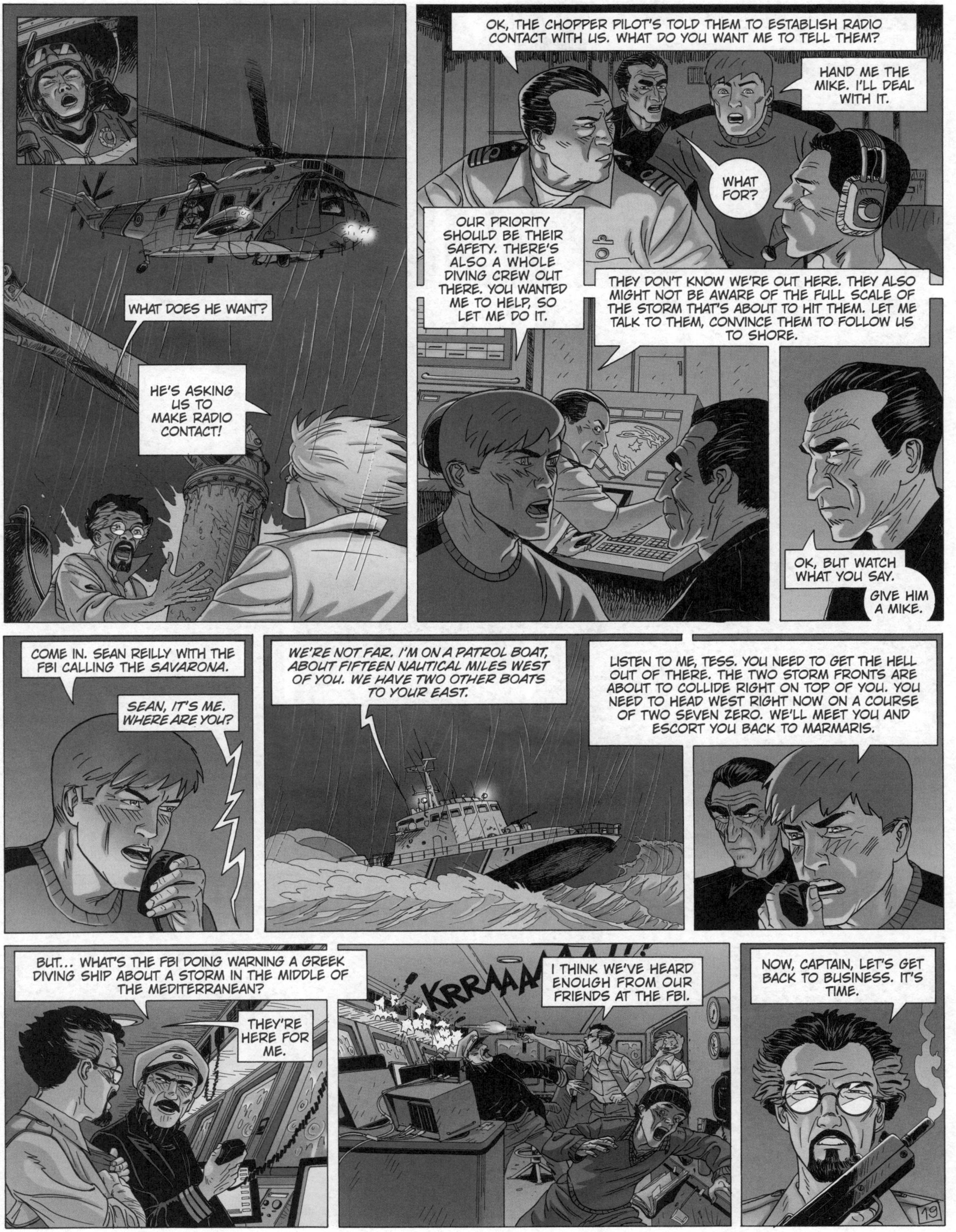
WHAT DOES HE WANT?
HE'S ASKING US TO MAKE RADIO CONTACT!
OK, THE CHOPPER PILOT'S TOLD THEM TO ESTABLISH RADIO CONTACT WITH US. WHAT DO YOU WANT ME TO TELL THEM?
HAND ME THE MIKE. I'LL DEAL WITH IT.
WHAT FOR?
OUR PRIORITY SHOULD BE THEIR SAFETY. THERE'S ALSO A WHOLE DIVING CREW OUT THERE. YOU WANTED ME TO HELP, SO LET ME DO IT.
THEY DON'T KNOW WE'RE OUT HERE. THEY ALSO MIGHT NOT BE AWARE OF THE FULL SCALE OF THE STORM THAT'S ABOUT TO HIT THEM. LET ME TALK TO THEM, CONVINCE THEM TO FOLLOW US TO SHORE.
OK, BUT WATCH WHAT YOU SAY.
GIVE HIM A MIKE.
COME IN. SEAN REILLY WITH THE FBI CALLING THE *SAVARONA*.
*SEAN, IT'S ME. WHERE ARE YOU?*
WE'RE NOT FAR. I'M ON A PATROL BOAT, ABOUT FIFTEEN NAUTICAL MILES WEST OF YOU. WE HAVE TWO OTHER BOATS TO YOUR EAST.
LISTEN TO ME, TESS. YOU NEED TO GET THE HELL OUT OF THERE. THE TWO STORM FRONTS ARE ABOUT TO COLLIDE RIGHT ON TOP OF YOU. YOU NEED TO HEAD WEST RIGHT NOW ON A COURSE OF TWO SEVEN ZERO. WE'LL MEET YOU AND ESCORT YOU BACK TO MARMARIS.
BUT... WHAT'S THE FBI DOING WARNING A GREEK DIVING SHIP ABOUT A STORM IN THE MIDDLE OF THE MEDITERRANEAN?
THEY'RE HERE FOR ME.
I THINK WE'VE HEARD ENOUGH FROM OUR FRIENDS AT THE FBI.
NOW, CAPTAIN, LET'S GET BACK TO BUSINESS. IT'S TIME.
19

WHAT... TESS? HELLO? THE SIGNAL'S GONE. THEY MUST'VE CUT THE RADIO.

SO WHAT? THEY DON'T HAVE TOO MANY OPTIONS.

THE STORMS HAVE THEM BOXED IN FROM THE NORTH AND THE SOUTH. THEY CAN EITHER HEAD EAST...

...WHERE TWO OF OUR PATROL BOATS ARE WAITING TO PICK THEM UP, OR WEST, TOWARD US.

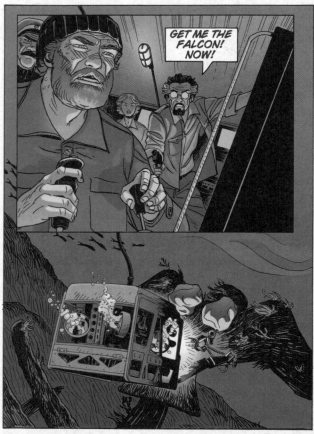

GET ME THE FALCON! NOW!

THIS IS GETTING OUT OF HAND! THE WIND'S ALMOST AT FIFTY KNOTS! IN THESE CONDITIONS, THERE ISN'T MUCH WE CAN DO ABOUT FORCING THEM TO FOLLOW US.

AS LONG AS THEY'RE THERE, WE KEEP ON!

BUT THIS IS MADNESS!

WHAT'S THE MATTER? CAN'T YOU HANDLE A FEW WAVES?

I DON'T SEE THEM TURNING TAIL AND RUNNING. THEY'RE NOT AFRAID TO BE OUT HERE. ARE YOU?!

THERE! AHEAD, TEN DEGREES TO STAR-BOARD! LOOK!

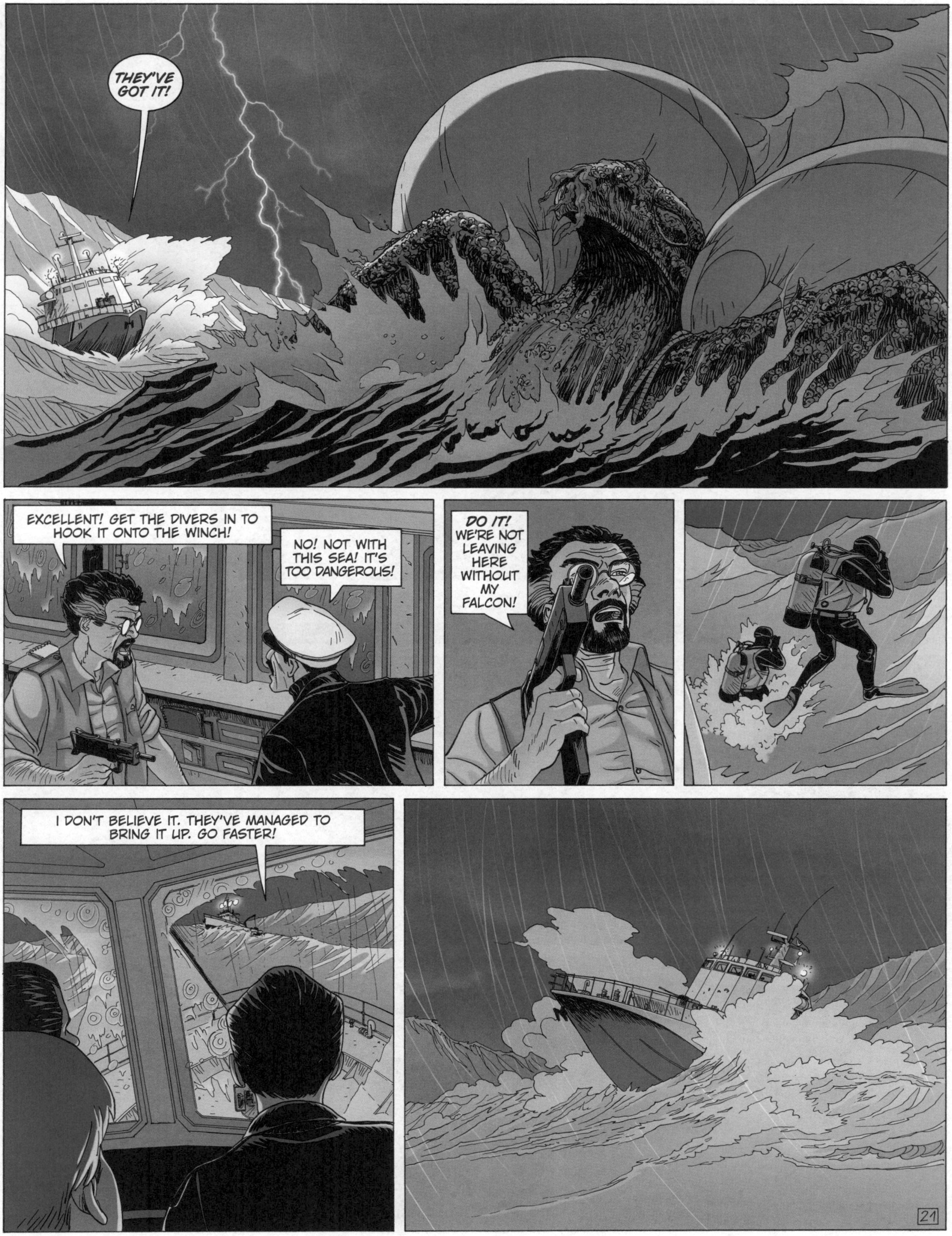
THEY'VE GOT IT!
EXCELLENT! GET THE DIVERS IN TO HOOK IT ONTO THE WINCH!
NO! NOT WITH THIS SEA! IT'S TOO DANGEROUS!
DO IT! WE'RE NOT LEAVING HERE WITHOUT MY FALCON!
I DON'T BELIEVE IT. THEY'VE MANAGED TO BRING IT UP. GO FASTER!
21

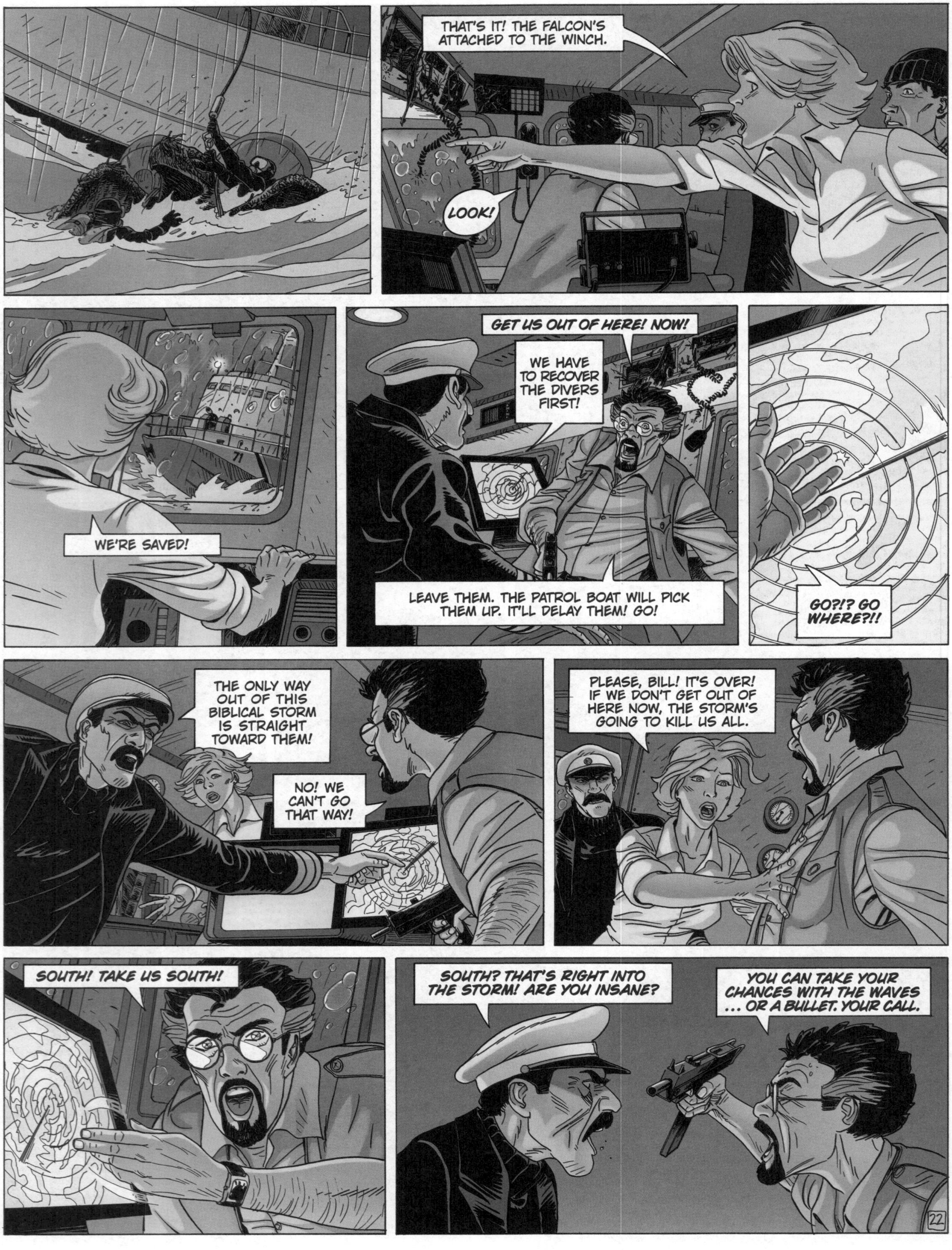
THAT'S IT! THE FALCON'S ATTACHED TO THE WINCH.
LOOK!
WE'RE SAVED!
GET US OUT OF HERE! NOW!
WE HAVE TO RECOVER THE DIVERS FIRST!
LEAVE THEM. THE PATROL BOAT WILL PICK THEM UP. IT'LL DELAY THEM! GO!
GO?!? GO WHERE?!!
THE ONLY WAY OUT OF THIS BIBLICAL STORM IS STRAIGHT TOWARD THEM!
NO! WE CAN'T GO THAT WAY!
PLEASE, BILL! IT'S OVER! IF WE DON'T GET OUT OF HERE NOW, THE STORM'S GOING TO KILL US ALL.
SOUTH! TAKE US SOUTH!
SOUTH? THAT'S RIGHT INTO THE STORM! ARE YOU INSANE?
YOU CAN TAKE YOUR CHANCES WITH THE WAVES ... OR A BULLET. YOUR CALL.
22

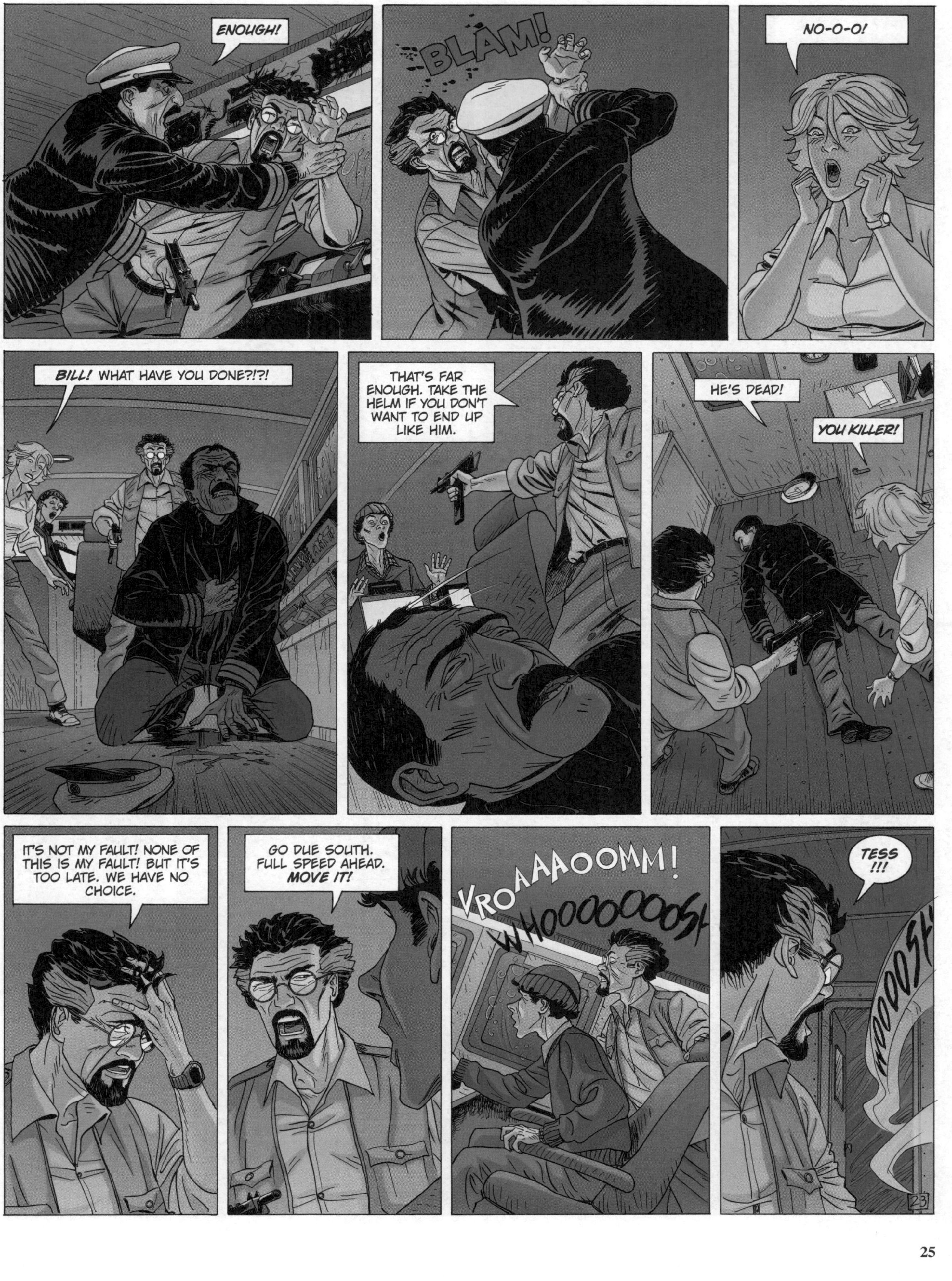
ENOUGH!
BLAM!
NO-O-O!
BILL! WHAT HAVE YOU DONE?!?!
THAT'S FAR ENOUGH. TAKE THE HELM IF YOU DON'T WANT TO END UP LIKE HIM.
HE'S DEAD!
YOU KILLER!
IT'S NOT MY FAULT! NONE OF THIS IS MY FAULT! BUT IT'S TOO LATE. WE HAVE NO CHOICE.
GO DUE SOUTH. FULL SPEED AHEAD. MOVE IT!
VROAAAOOMM!
WHOOOOOOOSH
TESS !!!
WOOOOSH
23

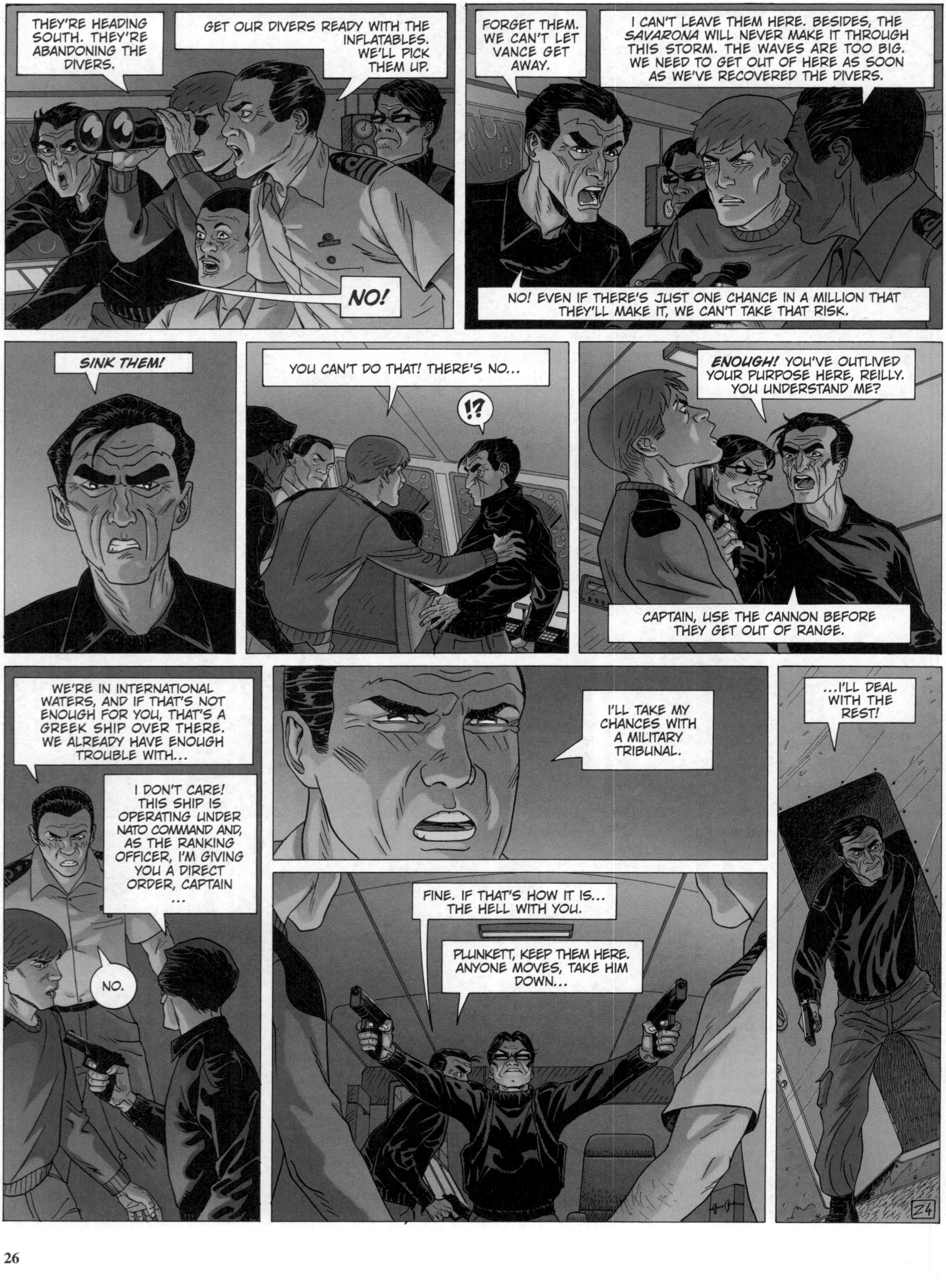

THEY'RE HEADING SOUTH. THEY'RE ABANDONING THE DIVERS.
GET OUR DIVERS READY WITH THE INFLATABLES. WE'LL PICK THEM UP.
NO!
FORGET THEM. WE CAN'T LET VANCE GET AWAY.
I CAN'T LEAVE THEM HERE. BESIDES, THE SAVARONA WILL NEVER MAKE IT THROUGH THIS STORM. THE WAVES ARE TOO BIG. WE NEED TO GET OUT OF HERE AS SOON AS WE'VE RECOVERED THE DIVERS.
NO! EVEN IF THERE'S JUST ONE CHANCE IN A MILLION THAT THEY'LL MAKE IT, WE CAN'T TAKE THAT RISK.
SINK THEM!
YOU CAN'T DO THAT! THERE'S NO...
!?
ENOUGH! YOU'VE OUTLIVED YOUR PURPOSE HERE, REILLY. YOU UNDERSTAND ME?
CAPTAIN, USE THE CANNON BEFORE THEY GET OUT OF RANGE.
WE'RE IN INTERNATIONAL WATERS, AND IF THAT'S NOT ENOUGH FOR YOU, THAT'S A GREEK SHIP OVER THERE. WE ALREADY HAVE ENOUGH TROUBLE WITH...
I DON'T CARE! THIS SHIP IS OPERATING UNDER NATO COMMAND AND, AS THE RANKING OFFICER, I'M GIVING YOU A DIRECT ORDER, CAPTAIN ...
NO.
I'LL TAKE MY CHANCES WITH A MILITARY TRIBUNAL.
FINE. IF THAT'S HOW IT IS... THE HELL WITH YOU.
PLUNKETT, KEEP THEM HERE. ANYONE MOVES, TAKE HIM DOWN...
...I'LL DEAL WITH THE REST!
24

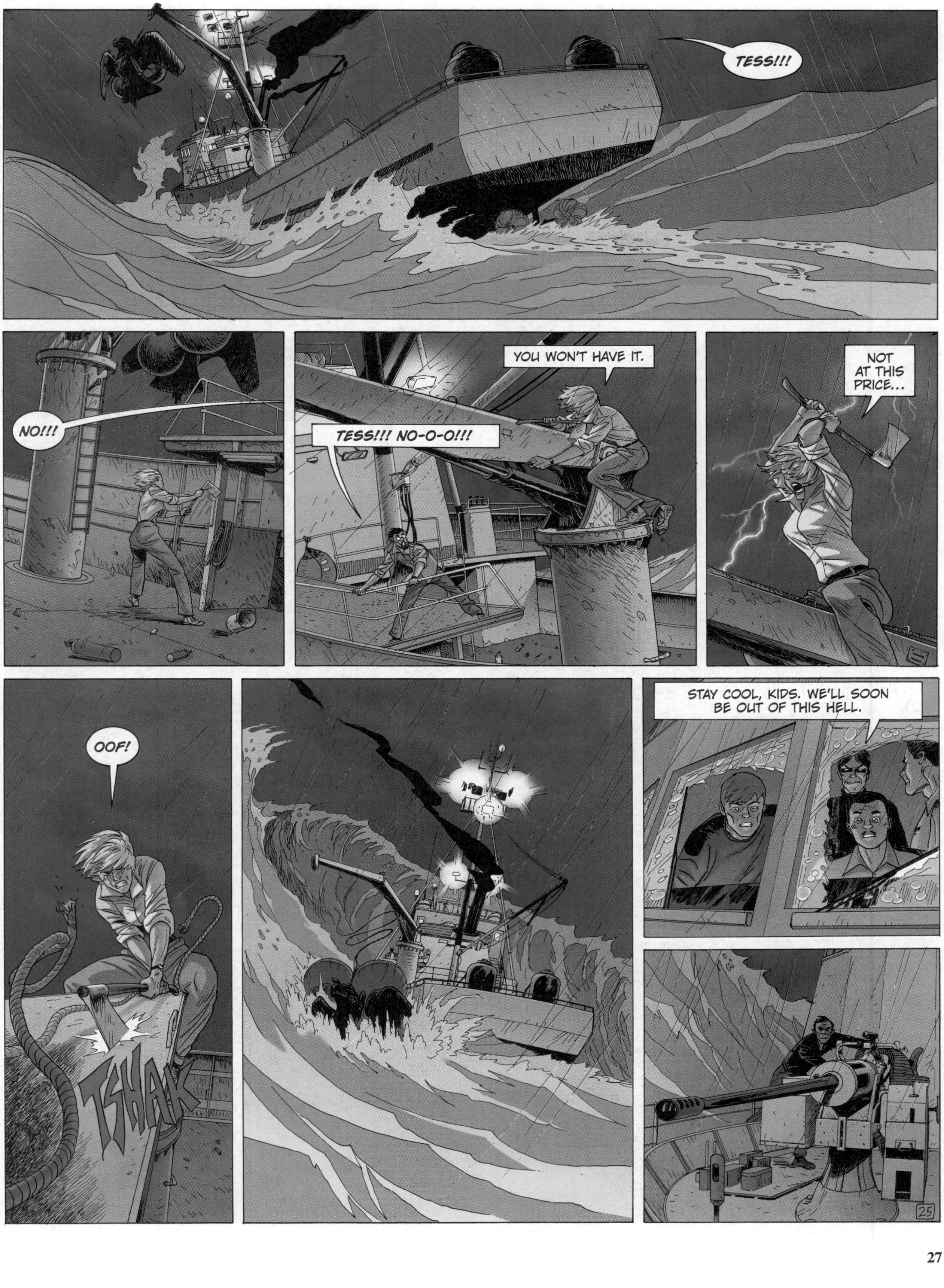
TESS!!!
NO!!!
YOU WON'T HAVE IT.
TESS!!! NO-O-O!!!
NOT AT THIS PRICE...
OOF!
TSHAK
STAY COOL, KIDS. WE'LL SOON BE OUT OF THIS HELL.
25

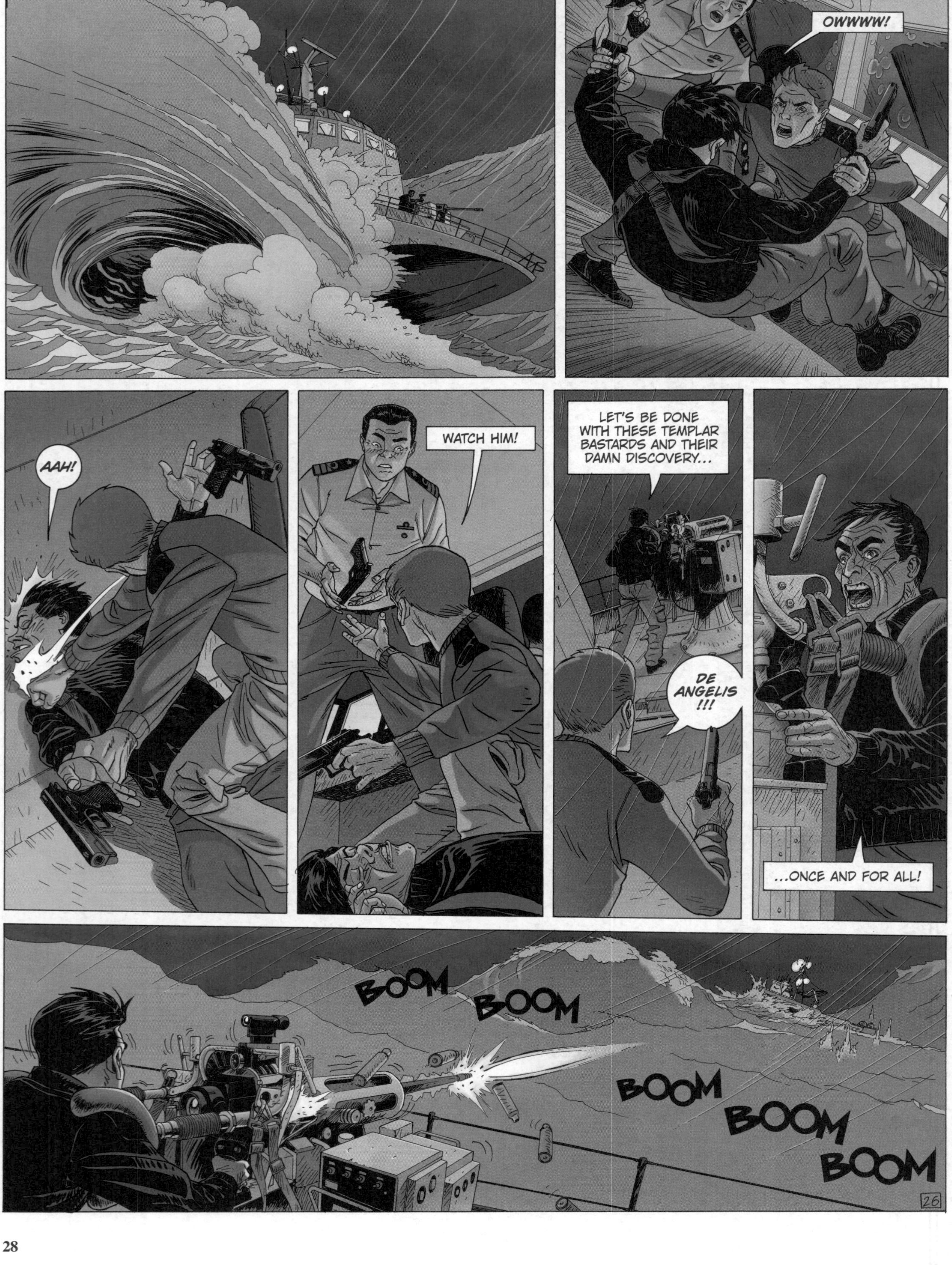
OWWWW!
AAH!
WATCH HIM!
LET'S BE DONE WITH THESE TEMPLAR BASTARDS AND THEIR DAMN DISCOVERY...
DE ANGELIS !!!
...ONCE AND FOR ALL!
BOOM
BOOM
BOOM
BOOM
BOOM
26

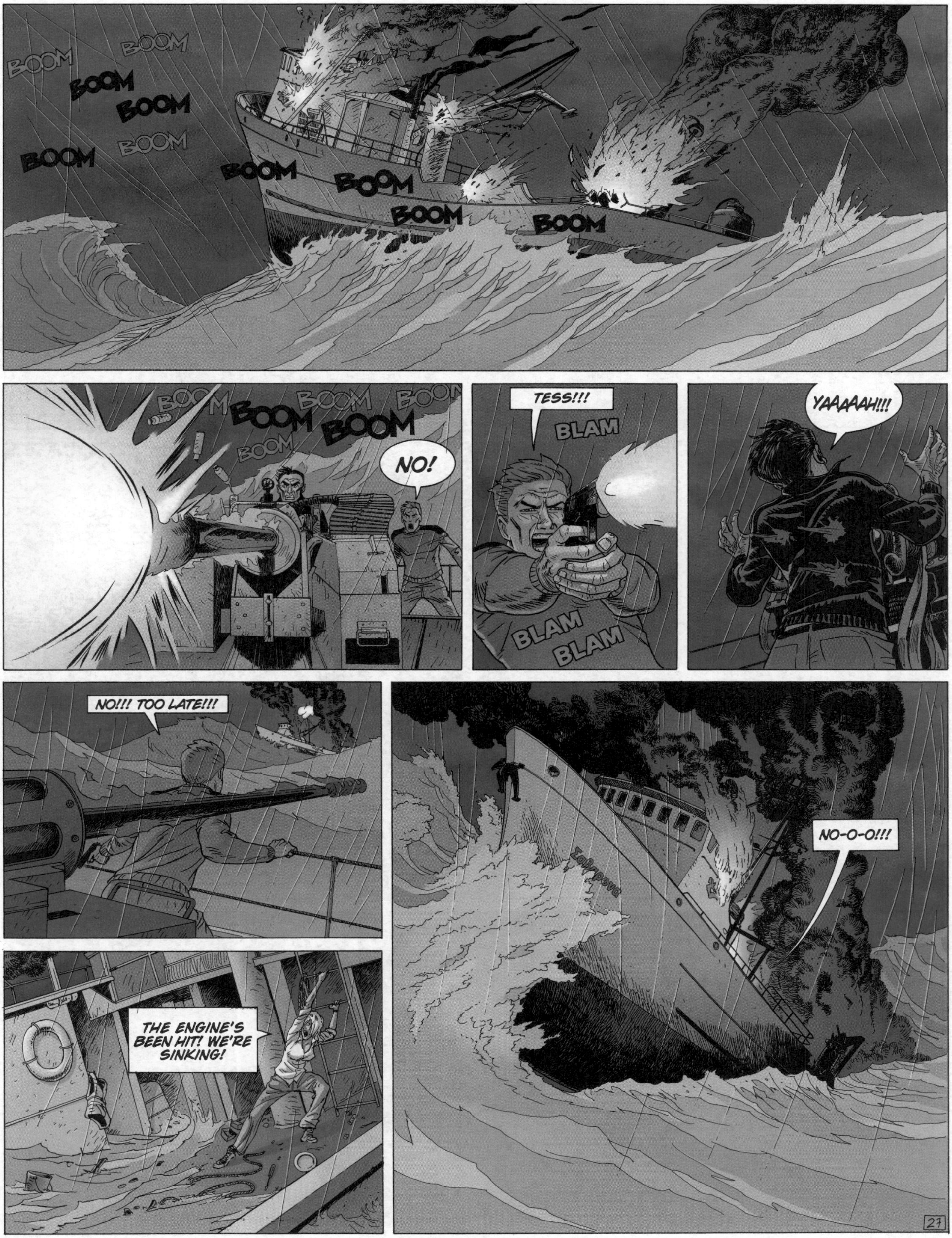
BOOM
BOOM
BOOM
BOOM
BOOM
BOOM
BOOM
BOOM
BOOM
BOOM
BOOM
BOOM
BOOM
BOOM
BOOM
BOOM
NO!
TESS!!!
BLAM
BLAM
BLAM
YAAAAAH!!!
NO!!! TOO LATE!!!
THE ENGINE'S BEEN HIT! WE'RE SINKING!
NO-O-O!!!
27

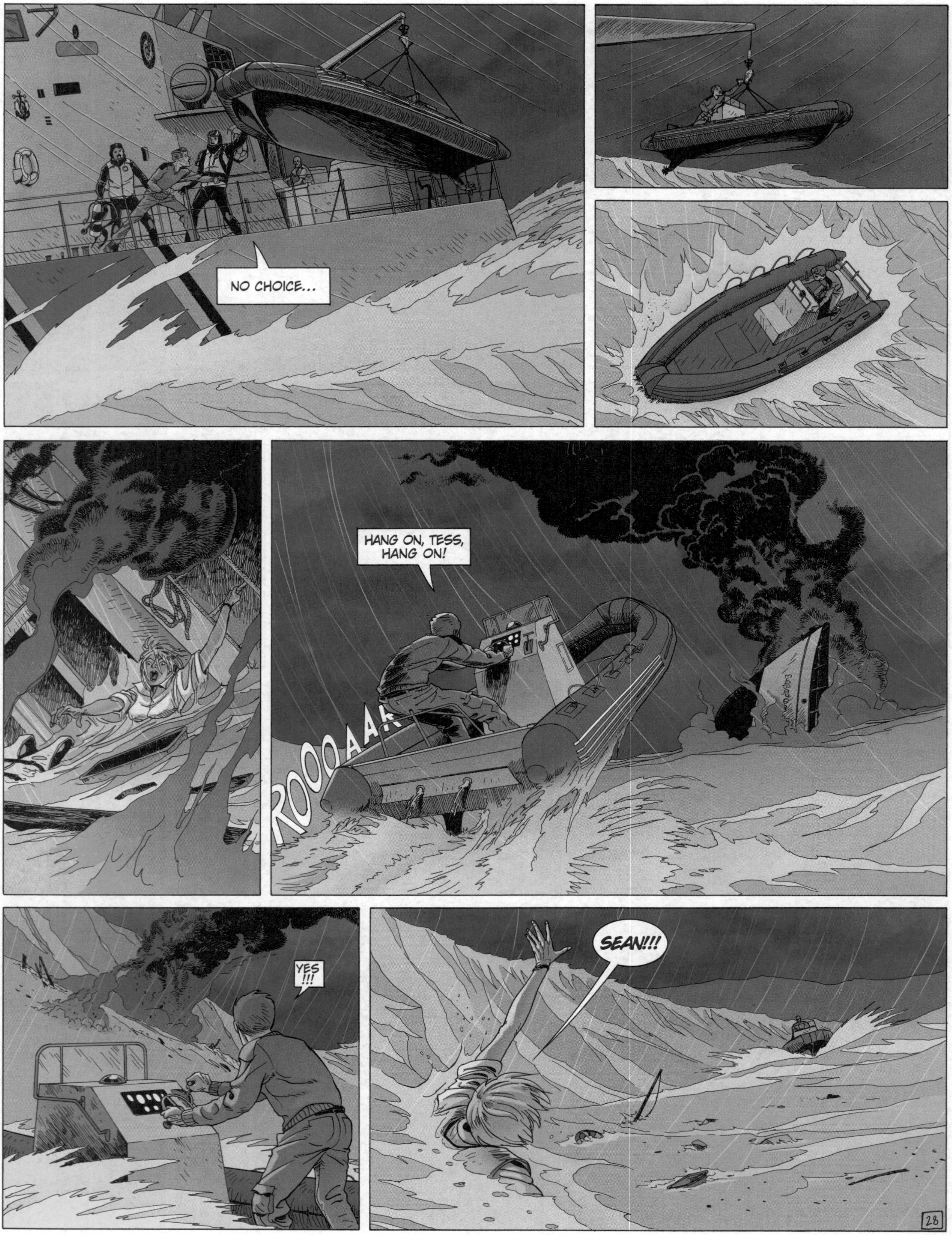
NO CHOICE...
HANG ON, TESS, HANG ON!
ROOOAAAR
YES !!!
SEAN!!!
28

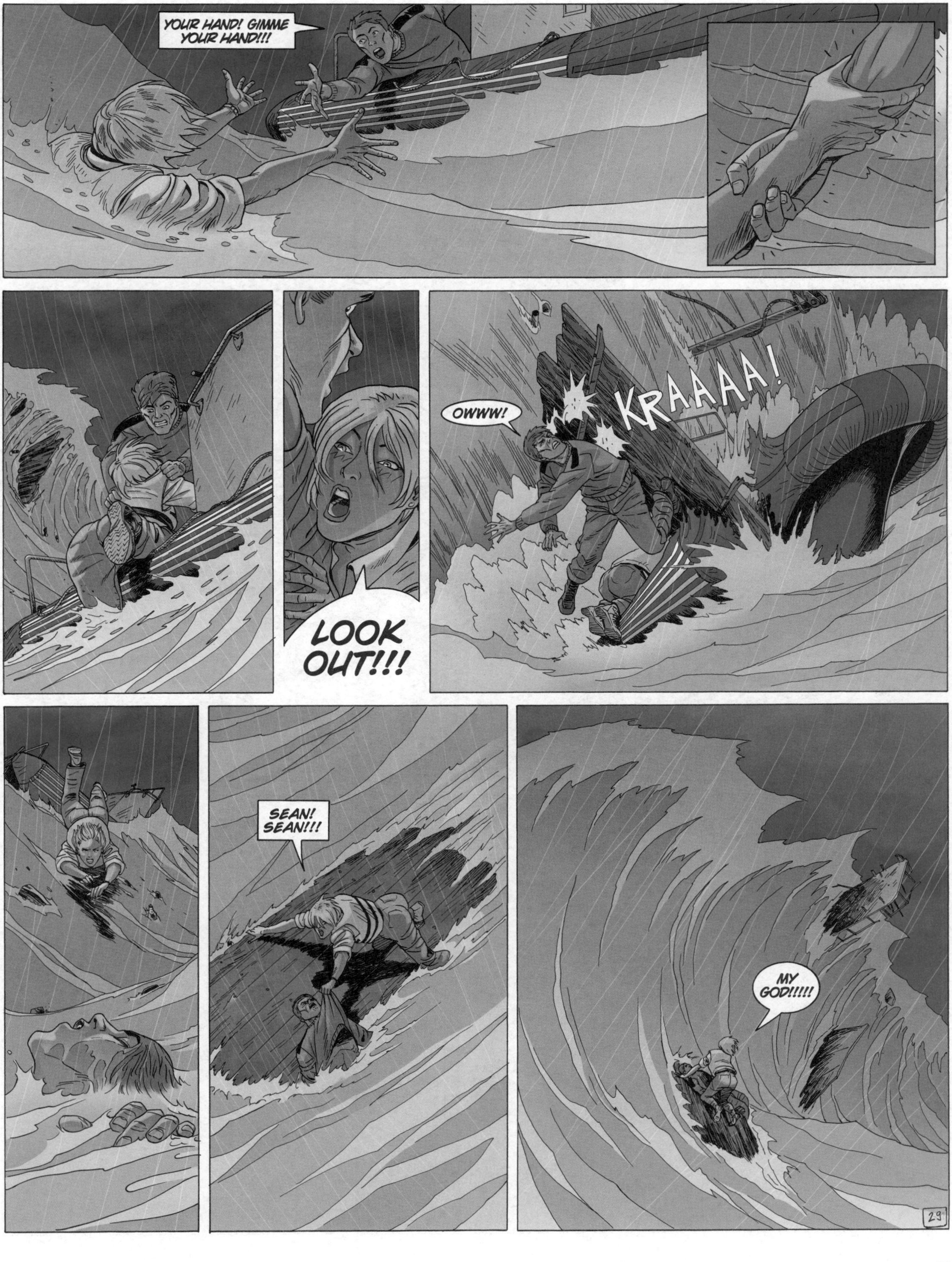
YOUR HAND! GIMME YOUR HAND!!!
LOOK OUT!!!
OWWW!
KRAAAA!
SEAN! SEAN!!!
MY GOD!!!!!
29

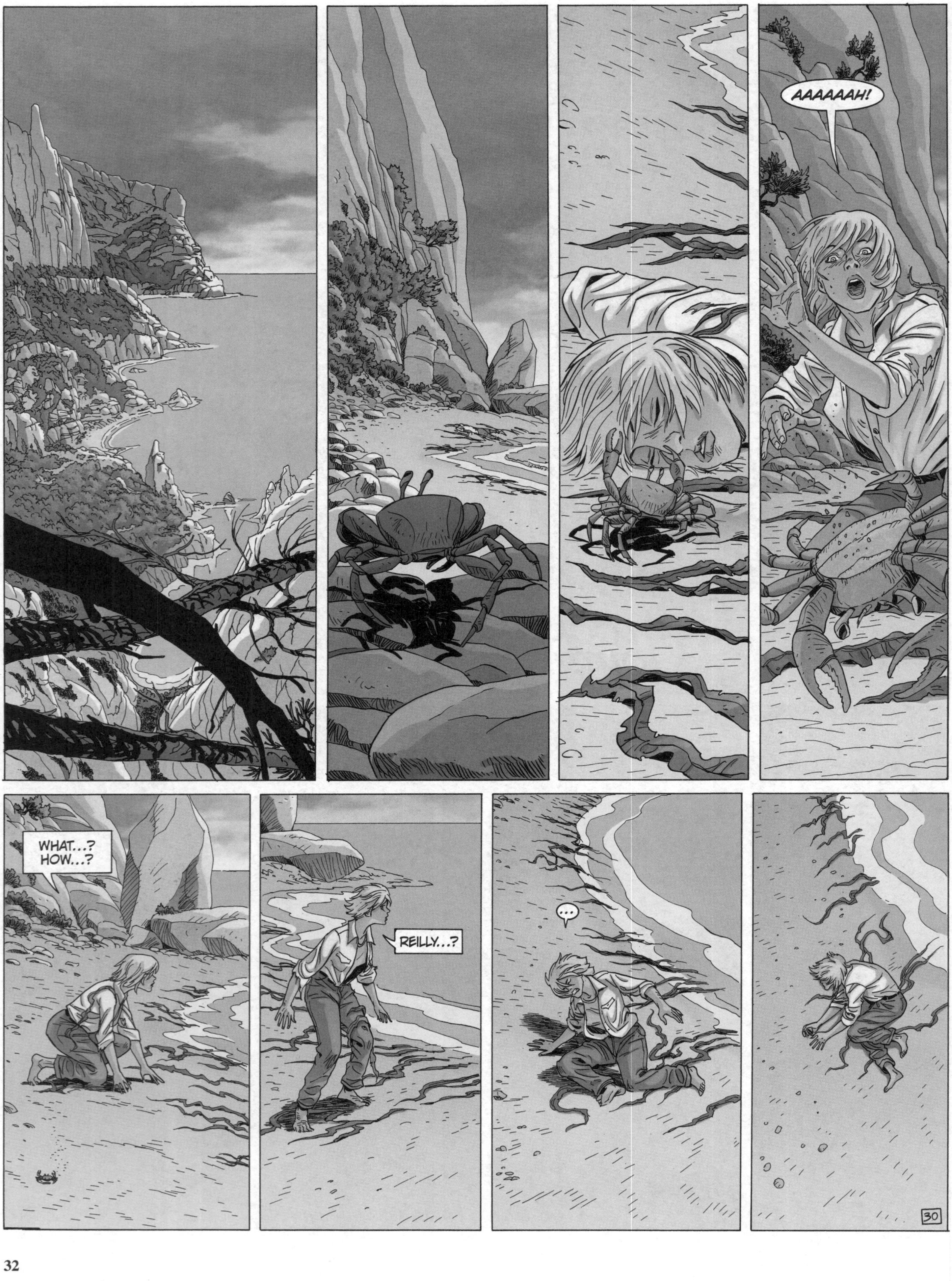
AAAAAAH!
WHAT...? HOW...?
REILLY...?
...
30

DOXA TO THEO. POS ESTHANESTE?*

I... I DON'T UNDERSTAND.

AH! YOU ARE ENGLISH?

AMERICAN.

WHAT HAPPENED TO YOU? YOU WERE FOUND ON THE BEACH...

I WAS ON A BOAT, WE HIT A STORM, AND...

*THANK GOD. HOW DO YOU FEEL? (GREEK)

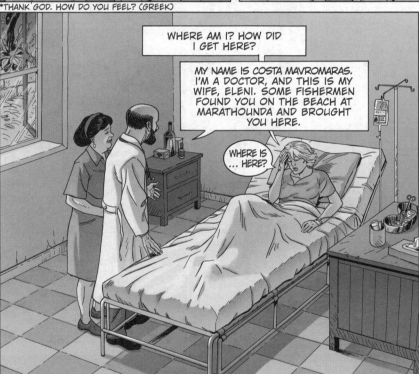

WHERE AM I? HOW DID I GET HERE?

MY NAME IS COSTA MAVROMARAS. I'M A DOCTOR, AND THIS IS MY WIFE, ELENI. SOME FISHERMEN FOUND YOU ON THE BEACH AT MARATHOUNDA AND BROUGHT YOU HERE.

WHERE IS ... HERE?

OUR HOUSE. IN OUR CLINIC. IN YIALOS.

YIALOS?

ON THE ISLAND OF SYMI. WHERE DID YOU THINK YOU WERE?

THERE WAS A MAN WITH ME... DID THE FISHERMEN FIND ANYONE ELSE?

YES, THEY FOUND SOMEONE, ON THE SAME BEACH AS YOU, BUT I'M AFRAID HIS STATE IS A BIT MORE SERIOUS THAN YOURS.

I NEED TO SEE HIM!

31

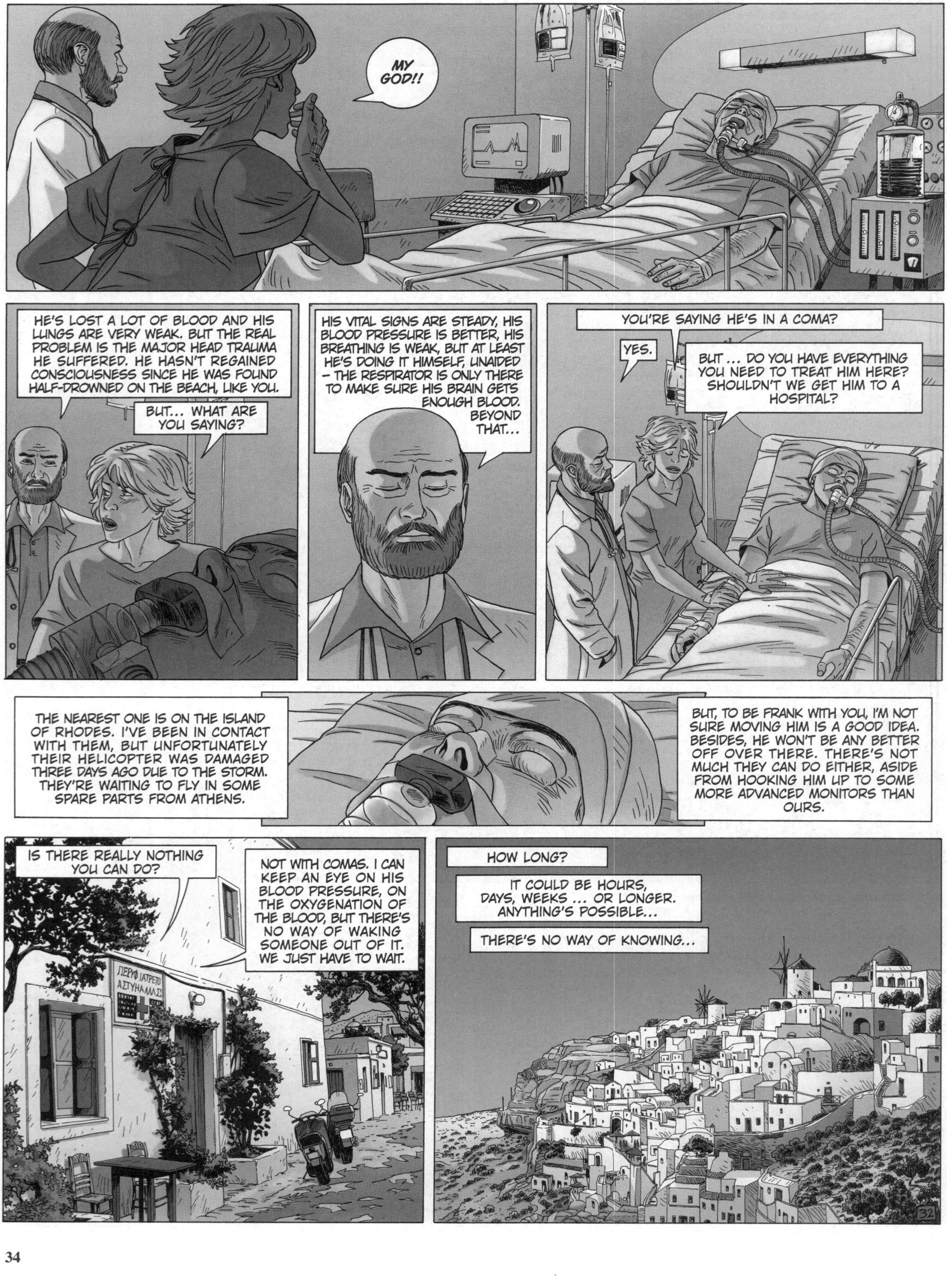
MY GOD!!
HE'S LOST A LOT OF BLOOD AND HIS LUNGS ARE VERY WEAK. BUT THE REAL PROBLEM IS THE MAJOR HEAD TRAUMA HE SUFFERED. HE HASN'T REGAINED CONSCIOUSNESS SINCE HE WAS FOUND HALF-DROWNED ON THE BEACH, LIKE YOU.
BUT... WHAT ARE YOU SAYING?
HIS VITAL SIGNS ARE STEADY, HIS BLOOD PRESSURE IS BETTER, HIS BREATHING IS WEAK, BUT AT LEAST HE'S DOING IT HIMSELF, UNAIDED – THE RESPIRATOR IS ONLY THERE TO MAKE SURE HIS BRAIN GETS ENOUGH BLOOD. BEYOND THAT...
YOU'RE SAYING HE'S IN A COMA?
YES.
BUT ... DO YOU HAVE EVERYTHING YOU NEED TO TREAT HIM HERE? SHOULDN'T WE GET HIM TO A HOSPITAL?
THE NEAREST ONE IS ON THE ISLAND OF RHODES. I'VE BEEN IN CONTACT WITH THEM, BUT UNFORTUNATELY THEIR HELICOPTER WAS DAMAGED THREE DAYS AGO DUE TO THE STORM. THEY'RE WAITING TO FLY IN SOME SPARE PARTS FROM ATHENS.
BUT, TO BE FRANK WITH YOU, I'M NOT SURE MOVING HIM IS A GOOD IDEA. BESIDES, HE WON'T BE ANY BETTER OFF OVER THERE. THERE'S NOT MUCH THEY CAN DO EITHER, ASIDE FROM HOOKING HIM UP TO SOME MORE ADVANCED MONITORS THAN OURS.
IS THERE REALLY NOTHING YOU CAN DO?
NOT WITH COMAS. I CAN KEEP AN EYE ON HIS BLOOD PRESSURE, ON THE OXYGENATION OF THE BLOOD, BUT THERE'S NO WAY OF WAKING SOMEONE OUT OF IT. WE JUST HAVE TO WAIT.
HOW LONG?
IT COULD BE HOURS, DAYS, WEEKS ... OR LONGER. ANYTHING'S POSSIBLE...
THERE'S NO WAY OF KNOWING...

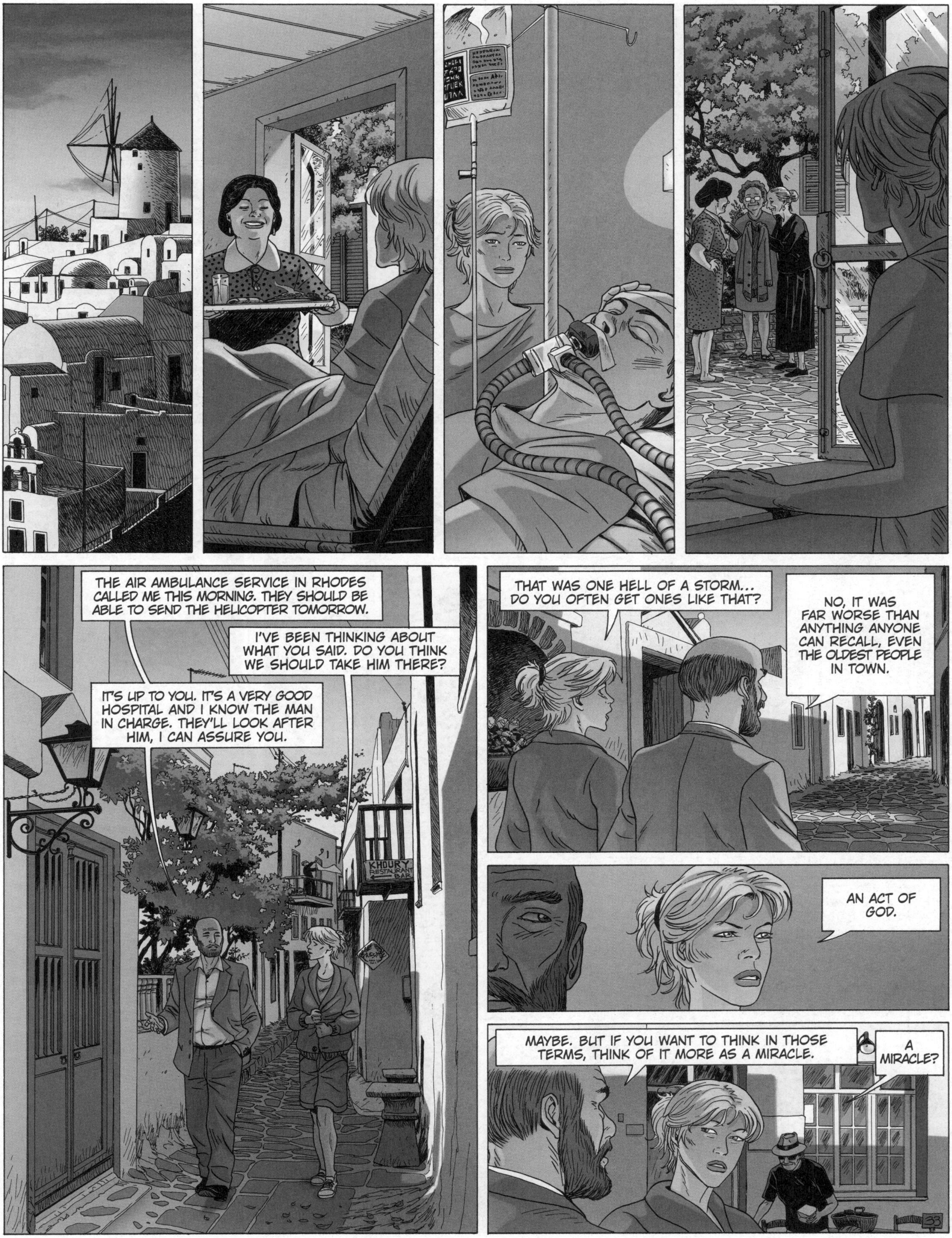
THE AIR AMBULANCE SERVICE IN RHODES CALLED ME THIS MORNING. THEY SHOULD BE ABLE TO SEND THE HELICOPTER TOMORROW.
I'VE BEEN THINKING ABOUT WHAT YOU SAID. DO YOU THINK WE SHOULD TAKE HIM THERE?
IT'S UP TO YOU. IT'S A VERY GOOD HOSPITAL AND I KNOW THE MAN IN CHARGE. THEY'LL LOOK AFTER HIM, I CAN ASSURE YOU.
KHOURY RESTAURANT BAR
THAT WAS ONE HELL OF A STORM... DO YOU OFTEN GET ONES LIKE THAT?
NO, IT WAS FAR WORSE THAN ANYTHING ANYONE CAN RECALL, EVEN THE OLDEST PEOPLE IN TOWN.
AN ACT OF GOD.
MAYBE. BUT IF YOU WANT TO THINK IN THOSE TERMS, THINK OF IT MORE AS A MIRACLE.
A MIRACLE?
33

YES. IT'S A MIRACLE THAT YOU AND YOUR FRIEND WERE WASHED ASHORE ON OUR LITTLE ISLAND. IT'S A BIG SEA OUT THERE. A BIT FURTHER NORTH AND YOU WOULD HAVE LANDED ON THE TURKISH COAST, WHICH, IN THIS AREA, IS ROCKY AND COMPLETELY DESERTED. THE TOWNS ARE ON THE OTHER SIDE OF THE PENINSULA. A BIT FURTHER SOUTH AND YOU WOULD HAVE MISSED OUR ISLAND ENTIRELY AND BEEN CARRIED OUT INTO THE AEGEAN SEA AND...

I HAVE TO GO. I'LL BE BACK THIS AFTERNOON.

ISN'T THERE ANYTHING I CAN DO TO HELP HIM?

YOUR FRIEND IS IN GOOD HANDS. EVEN IF OUR CLINIC ISN'T ANYTHING LIKE THE HOSPITALS YOU'RE USED TO IN AMERICA, WE'VE HAD A LOT OF EXPERIENCE TREATING ALL KINDS OF INJURIES. EVEN ON A SMALL ISLAND LIKE THIS, PEOPLE DO GET HURT.

BY THE WAY... HAVE YOU TALKED TO HIM YET?

TO REILLY?

OF COURSE. YOU SHOULD. TALK TO HIM. GIVE HIM STRENGTH.

YOU MUST THINK YOU'VE FALLEN ON SOME SMALL-TOWN WITCH DOCTOR. I PROMISE YOU THAT'S NOT THE CASE. MANY STUDIES BY PROMINENT PHYSICIANS SUPPORT THE IDEA. JUST BECAUSE HE'S IN A COMA DOESN'T MEAN HE CAN'T HEAR. IT JUST MEANS HE CAN'T RESPOND ... YET.

TALK TO HIM ... AND PRAY FOR HIS RECOVERY.

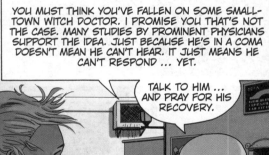

I'M NOT VERY GOOD AT THAT.

IN YOUR OWN WAY, ALTHOUGH YOU DON'T REALISE IT, YOU'RE ALREADY DOING IT. YOU'RE PRAYING FOR HIM JUST BY WISHING HE WOULD RECOVER... A LOT OF PRAYERS ARE BEING SAID FOR HIM.

MANY OF THE MEN ON THIS ISLAND EARN THEIR LIVING FROM THE SEA. THERE WERE FOUR FISHING BOATS OUT AT SEA THE NIGHT THE STORM HIT. THEIR FAMILIES PRAYED TO GOD AND TO THE ARCHANGEL MICHAEL. NOW, MORE PRAYERS ARE BEING SAID, PRAYERS OF THANKS. AND PRAYERS FOR YOUR FRIEND'S RECOVERY.

THEY'RE PRAY-ING FOR HIS RECOVERY?

WE ALL ARE.

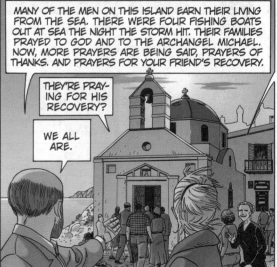

BUT YOU DON'T EVEN KNOW HIM.

IT DOESN'T MATTER. THE SEA BROUGHT HIM TO US, AND IT'S OUR DUTY TO NURSE HIM BACK TO HEALTH SO HE CAN GO ON WITH HIS LIFE.

NOW I REALLY MUST GO...

THE BEACH ... WHERE I WAS FOUND... I'D LIKE TO SEE IT.

IT'S BEYOND THE SMALL SET-TLEMENT AT MARATHOUNDA, NEAR THE MONASTERY AT PANORMITIS. COME. ONE OF THE FISHERMEN WHO FOUND YOU WILL TAKE YOU...

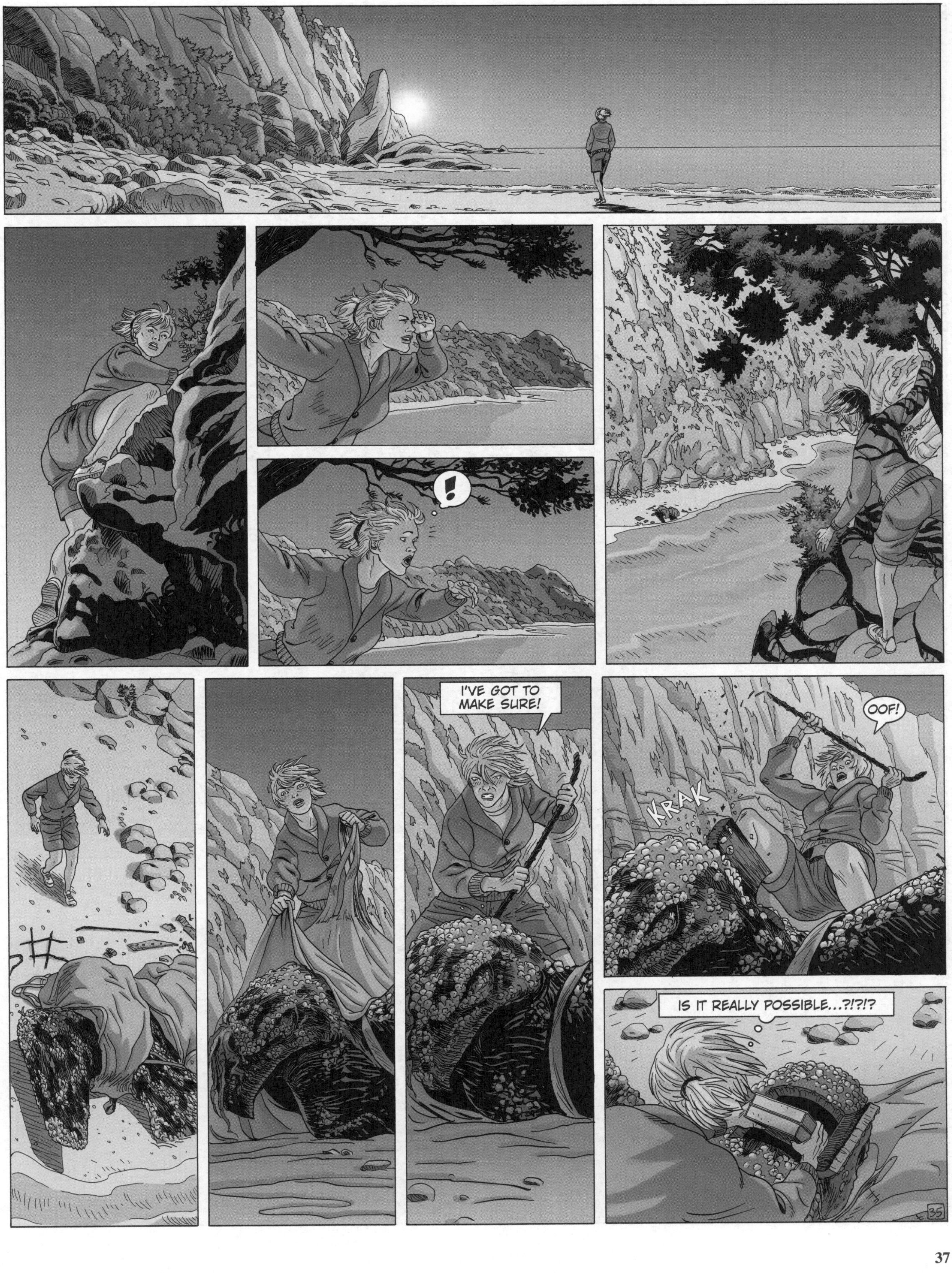
!
I'VE GOT TO MAKE SURE!
KRAK
OOF!
IS IT REALLY POSSIBLE...?!?!?
35

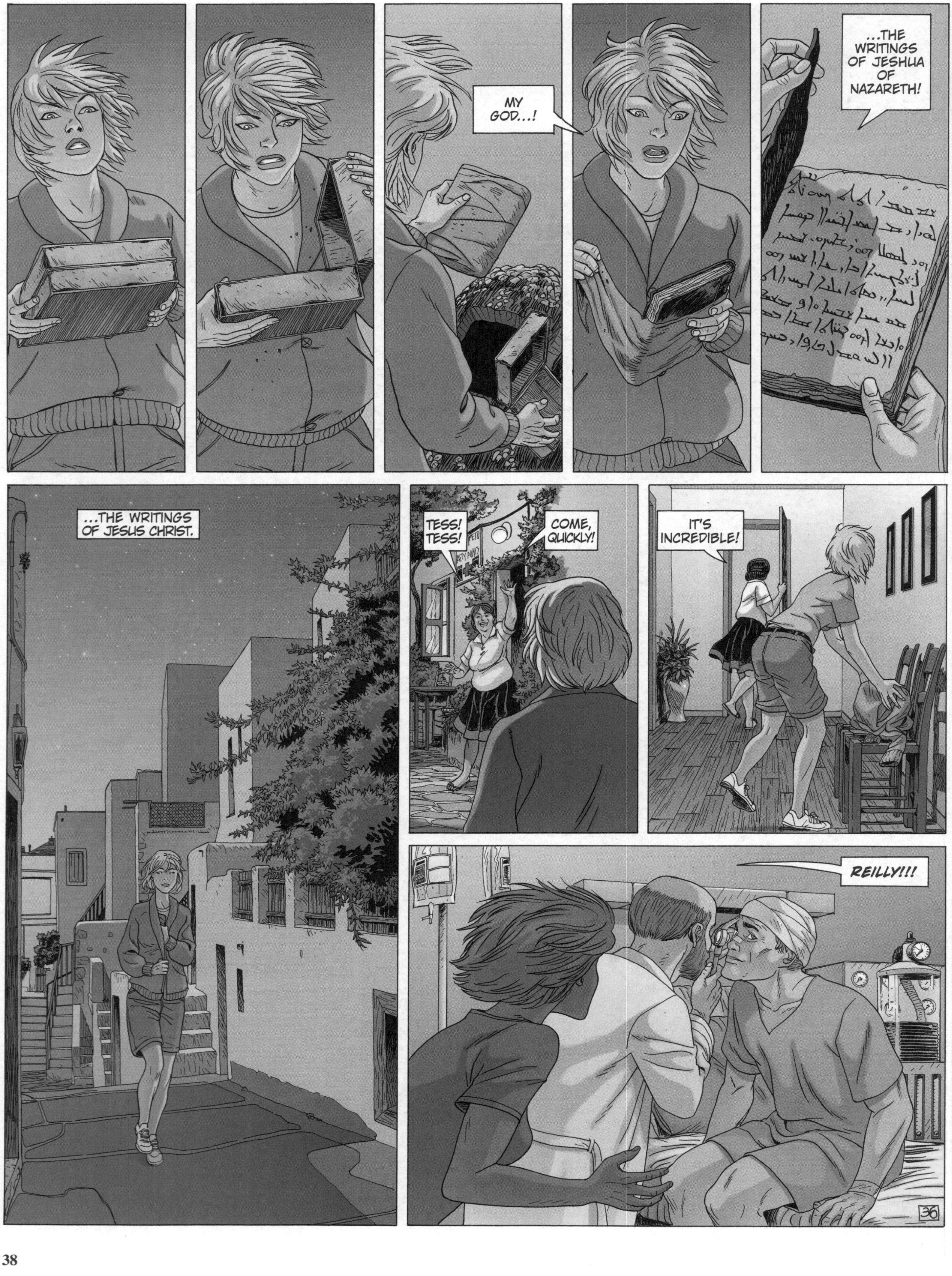
MY GOD...!
...THE WRITINGS OF JESHUA OF NAZARETH!
...THE WRITINGS OF JESUS CHRIST.
TESS! TESS!
COME, QUICKLY!
IT'S INCREDIBLE!
REILLY!!!
36

I'M SORRY ... FOR EVERYTHING. I DON'T KNOW WHAT CAME OVER ME. I MUST HAVE BEEN OUT OF MY MIND, LEAVING YOU IN THE MOUNTAINS LIKE THAT... THIS WHOLE MESS...

LET'S NOT TALK ABOUT IT... WE BOTH MADE IT, AND THAT'S THE MAIN THING, ISN'T IT?

ARE YOU GONNA BE OKAY?

IT'S WEIRD, BUT THIS WHOLE THING, TURKEY, THE VATICAN, THE STORM... IT JUST FEELS LIKE A BAD DREAM. MAYBE I'M TOO DRUGGED UP OR SOMETHING, BUT... I'M SURE IT'LL HIT HOME AT SOME POINT. RIGHT NOW, I'M SO TIRED I JUST FEEL COMPLETELY DRAINED. BUT I DON'T KNOW HOW MUCH OF IT IS PHYSICAL AND HOW MUCH OF IT IS ... SOMETHING ELSE.

VANCE AND DE ANGELIS GOT WHAT THEY DESERVED, AND YOU'RE ALIVE. THERE'S CAUSE FOR FAITH IN THAT, ISN'T THERE?

MAYBE...

WHAT HAVE YOU GOT THERE?

SOMETHING I NEED TO SHOW YOU.

BUT... WHERE'D YOU FIND IT?

IN THE FALCON, A COUPLE OF BAYS DOWN FROM WHERE WE WERE FOUND. THE LIFT BAGS WERE STILL ATTACHED TO IT.

SO, WHAT DO YOU THINK? IS IT REAL?

I DON'T KNOW. IT DEFINITELY LOOKS RIGHT, BUT YOU CAN'T REALLY TELL WITHOUT SENDING IT TO A LAB. THERE ARE MANY TESTS WE'D HAVE TO RUN ON IT: CARBON DATING, ANALYSING THE COMPOSITION OF THE PAPER AND THE INK, CHECKING FOR CALLIGRAPHIC CONSISTENCY...

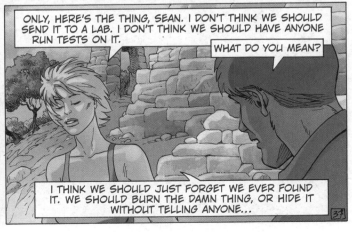

ONLY, HERE'S THE THING, SEAN. I DON'T THINK WE SHOULD SEND IT TO A LAB. I DON'T THINK WE SHOULD HAVE ANYONE RUN TESTS ON IT.

WHAT DO YOU MEAN?

I THINK WE SHOULD JUST FORGET WE EVER FOUND IT. WE SHOULD BURN THE DAMN THING, OR HIDE IT WITHOUT TELLING ANYONE...

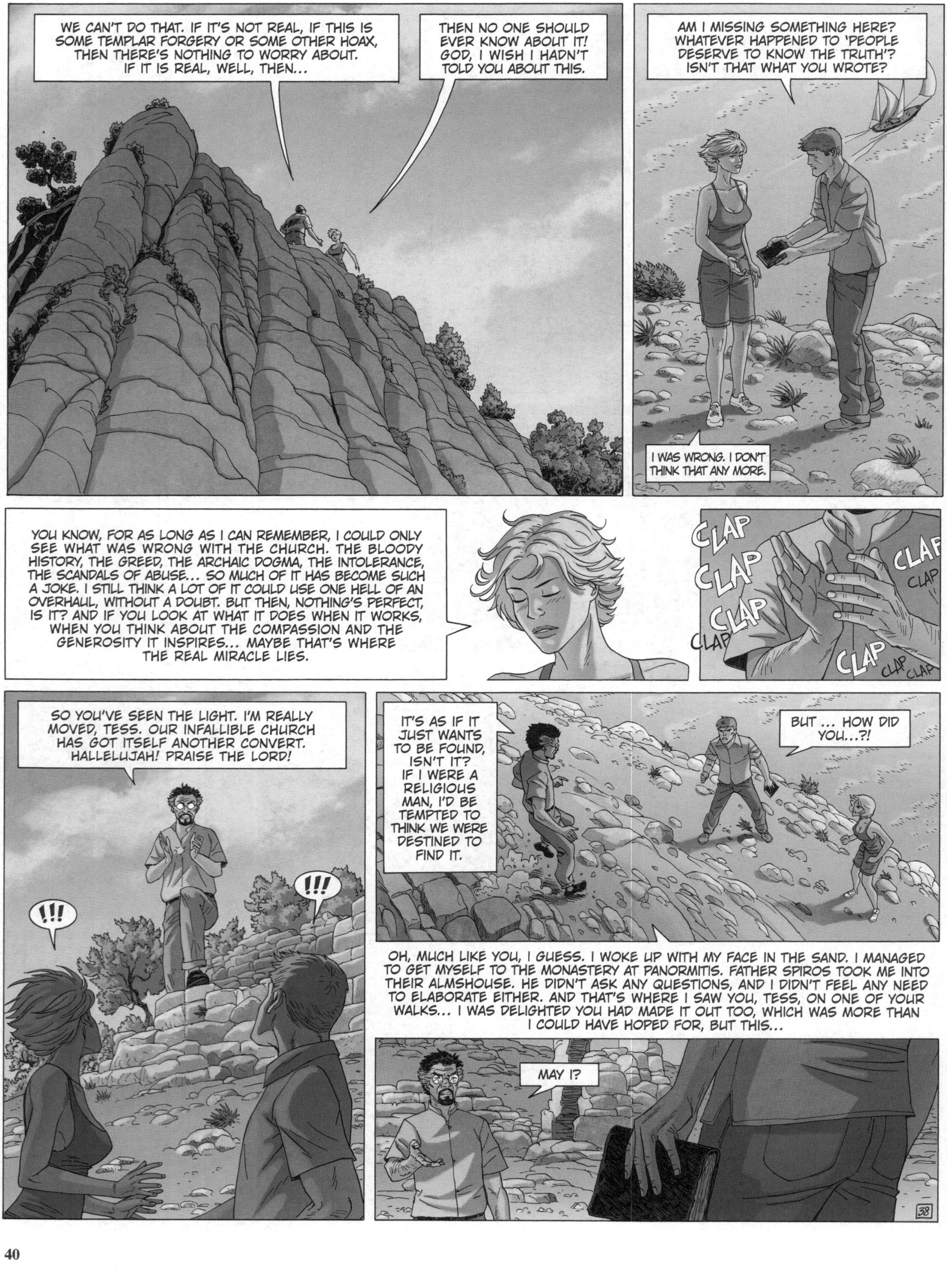

WE CAN'T DO THAT. IF IT'S NOT REAL, IF THIS IS SOME TEMPLAR FORGERY OR SOME OTHER HOAX, THEN THERE'S NOTHING TO WORRY ABOUT. IF IT IS REAL, WELL, THEN...
THEN NO ONE SHOULD EVER KNOW ABOUT IT! GOD, I WISH I HADN'T TOLD YOU ABOUT THIS.
AM I MISSING SOMETHING HERE? WHATEVER HAPPENED TO 'PEOPLE DESERVE TO KNOW THE TRUTH'? ISN'T THAT WHAT YOU WROTE?
I WAS WRONG. I DON'T THINK THAT ANY MORE.
YOU KNOW, FOR AS LONG AS I CAN REMEMBER, I COULD ONLY SEE WHAT WAS WRONG WITH THE CHURCH. THE BLOODY HISTORY, THE GREED, THE ARCHAIC DOGMA, THE INTOLERANCE, THE SCANDALS OF ABUSE... SO MUCH OF IT HAS BECOME SUCH A JOKE. I STILL THINK A LOT OF IT COULD USE ONE HELL OF AN OVERHAUL, WITHOUT A DOUBT. BUT THEN, NOTHING'S PERFECT, IS IT? AND IF YOU LOOK AT WHAT IT DOES WHEN IT WORKS, WHEN YOU THINK ABOUT THE COMPASSION AND THE GENEROSITY IT INSPIRES... MAYBE THAT'S WHERE THE REAL MIRACLE LIES.
CLAP CLAP CLAP CLAP CLAP CLAP CLAP CLAP CLAP CLAP
SO YOU'VE SEEN THE LIGHT. I'M REALLY MOVED, TESS. OUR INFALLIBLE CHURCH HAS GOT ITSELF ANOTHER CONVERT. HALLELUJAH! PRAISE THE LORD!
!!!
!!!
IT'S AS IF IT JUST WANTS TO BE FOUND, ISN'T IT? IF I WERE A RELIGIOUS MAN, I'D BE TEMPTED TO THINK WE WERE DESTINED TO FIND IT.
BUT ... HOW DID YOU...?!
OH, MUCH LIKE YOU, I GUESS. I WOKE UP WITH MY FACE IN THE SAND. I MANAGED TO GET MYSELF TO THE MONASTERY AT PANORMITIS. FATHER SPIROS TOOK ME INTO THEIR ALMSHOUSE. HE DIDN'T ASK ANY QUESTIONS, AND I DIDN'T FEEL ANY NEED TO ELABORATE EITHER. AND THAT'S WHERE I SAW YOU, TESS, ON ONE OF YOUR WALKS... I WAS DELIGHTED YOU HAD MADE IT OUT TOO, WHICH WAS MORE THAN I COULD HAVE HOPED FOR, BUT THIS...
MAY I?
38

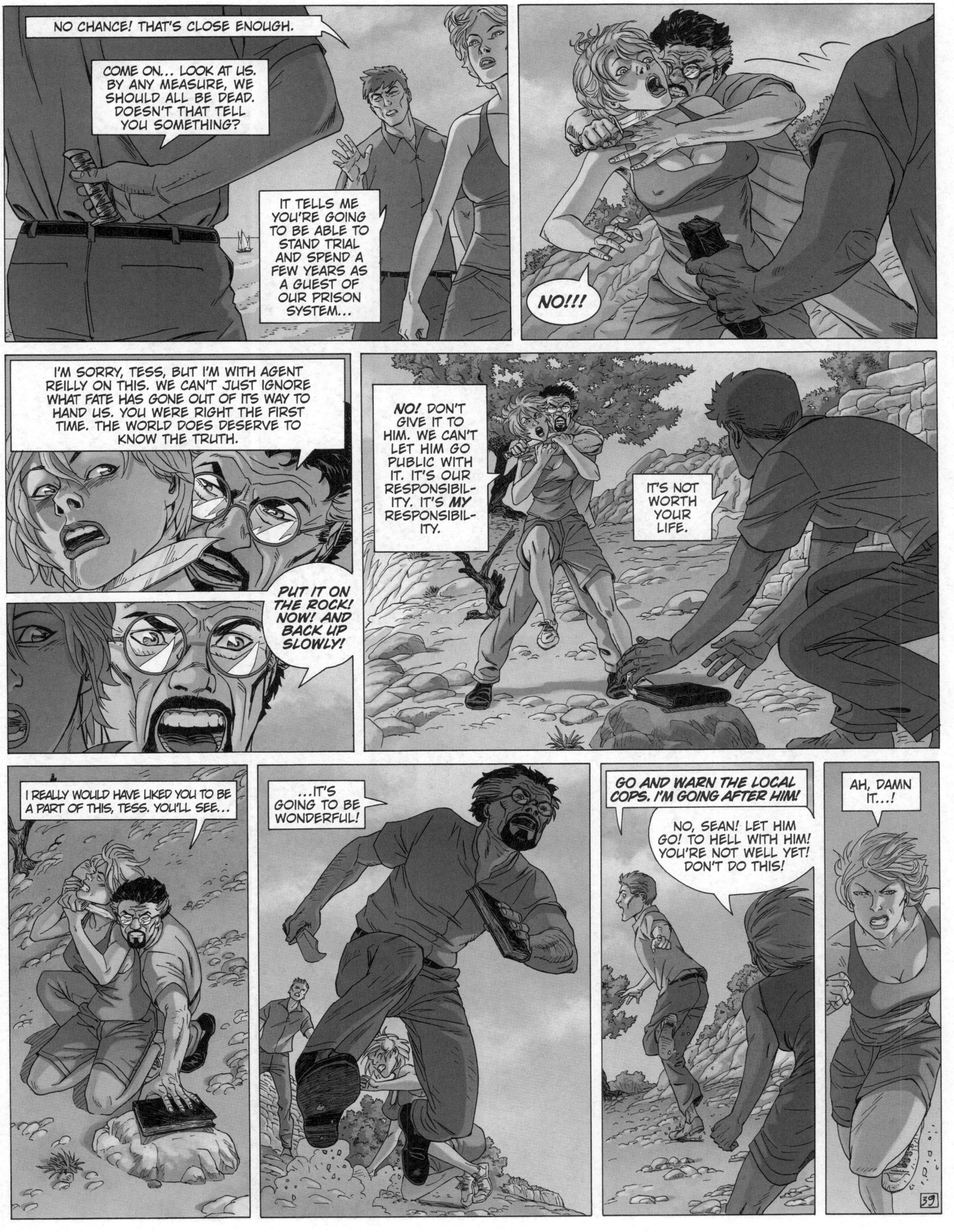

NO CHANCE! THAT'S CLOSE ENOUGH.
COME ON... LOOK AT US. BY ANY MEASURE, WE SHOULD ALL BE DEAD. DOESN'T THAT TELL YOU SOMETHING?
IT TELLS ME YOU'RE GOING TO BE ABLE TO STAND TRIAL AND SPEND A FEW YEARS AS A GUEST OF OUR PRISON SYSTEM...
NO!!!
I'M SORRY, TESS, BUT I'M WITH AGENT REILLY ON THIS. WE CAN'T JUST IGNORE WHAT FATE HAS GONE OUT OF ITS WAY TO HAND US. YOU WERE RIGHT THE FIRST TIME. THE WORLD DOES DESERVE TO KNOW THE TRUTH.
PUT IT ON THE ROCK! NOW! AND BACK UP SLOWLY!
NO! DON'T GIVE IT TO HIM. WE CAN'T LET HIM GO PUBLIC WITH IT. IT'S OUR RESPONSIBILITY. IT'S MY RESPONSIBILITY.
IT'S NOT WORTH YOUR LIFE.
I REALLY WOULD HAVE LIKED YOU TO BE A PART OF THIS, TESS. YOU'LL SEE...
...IT'S GOING TO BE WONDERFUL!
GO AND WARN THE LOCAL COPS. I'M GOING AFTER HIM!
NO, SEAN! LET HIM GO! TO HELL WITH HIM! YOU'RE NOT WELL YET! DON'T DO THIS!
AH, DAMN IT...!
39

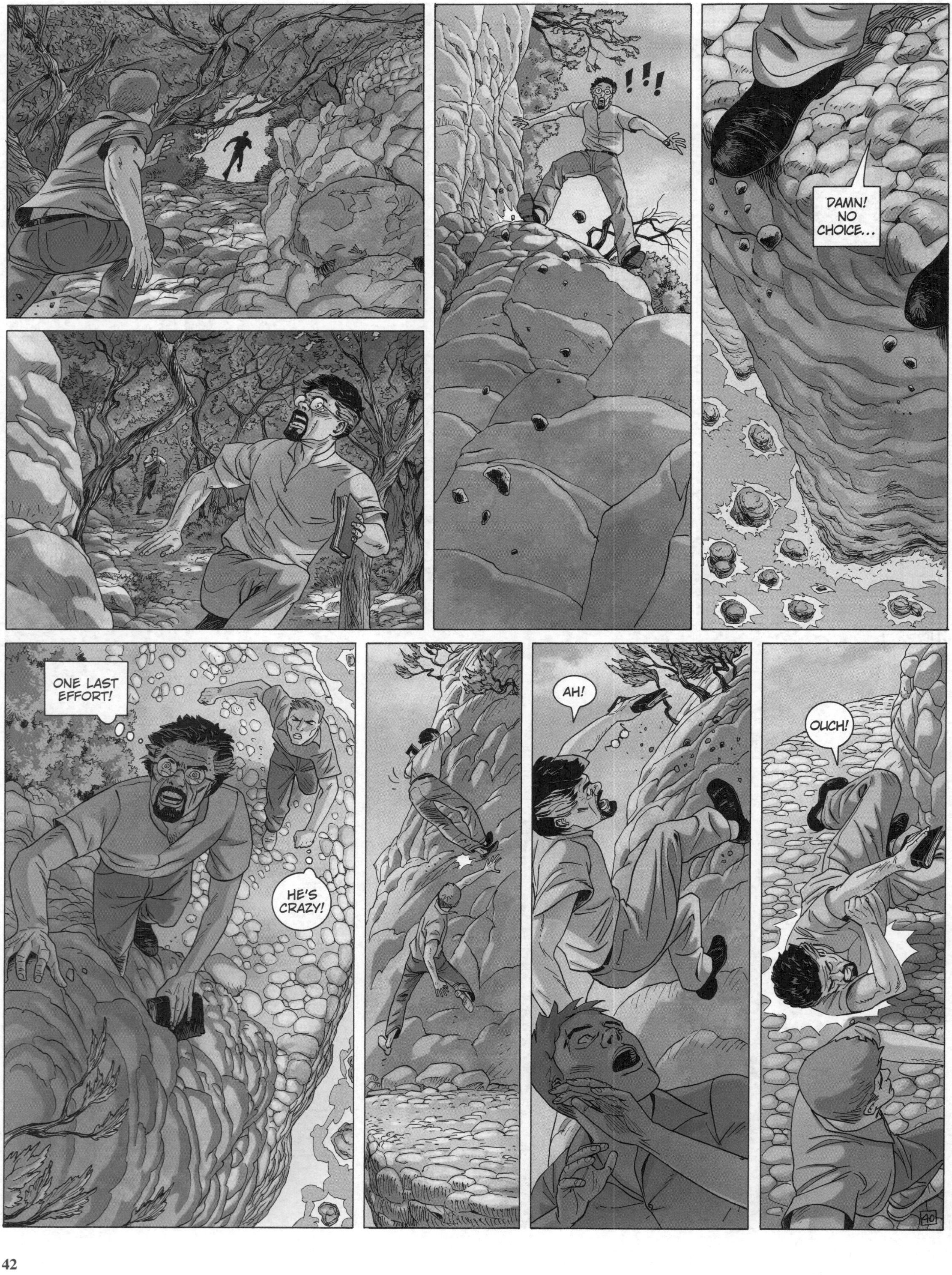
!!!
DAMN! NO CHOICE...
ONE LAST EFFORT!
HE'S CRAZY!
AH!
OUCH!
40

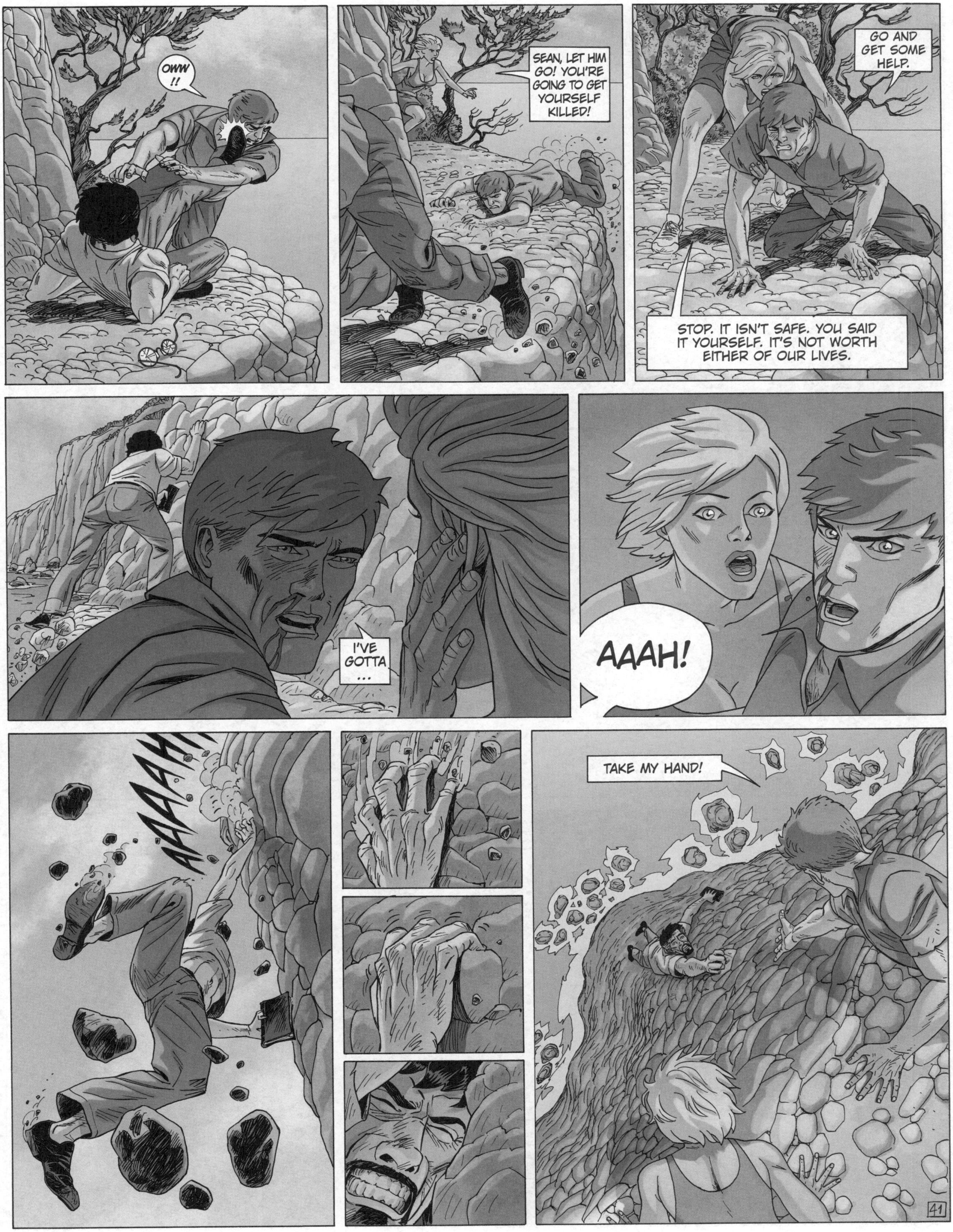

OWW !!
SEAN, LET HIM GO! YOU'RE GOING TO GET YOURSELF KILLED!
GO AND GET SOME HELP.
STOP. IT ISN'T SAFE. YOU SAID IT YOURSELF. IT'S NOT WORTH EITHER OF OUR LIVES.
I'VE GOTTA ...
AAAH!
AAAAAH!
TAKE MY HAND!
41

I CAN'T! TAKE THE CODEX! I...

OW!

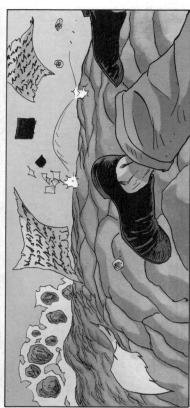

NO-O-O!!!

IT'S OVER... NOW WE'LL NEVER KNOW THE TRUTH...

GOOD.

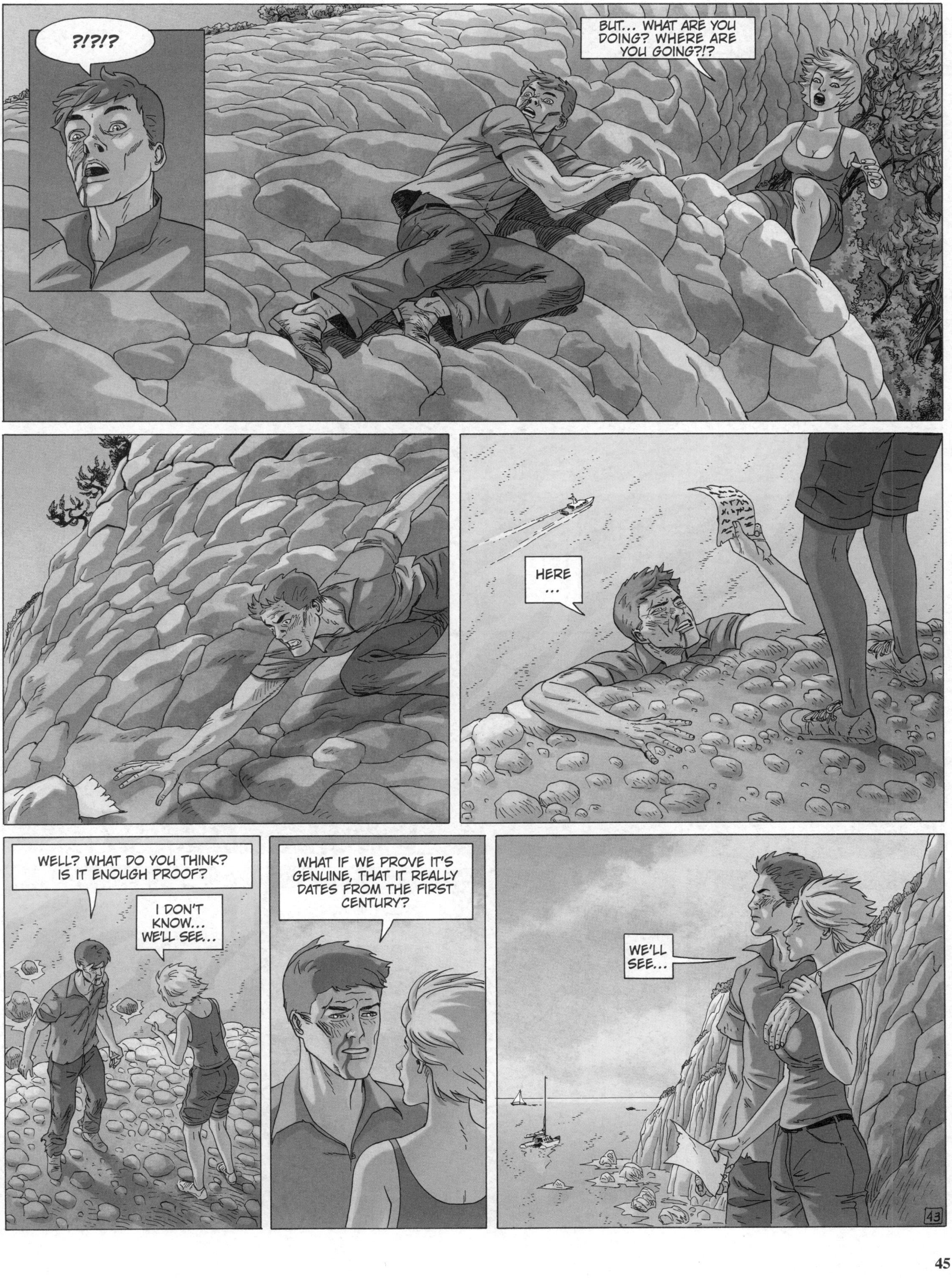
?!?!?
BUT... WHAT ARE YOU DOING? WHERE ARE YOU GOING?!?
HERE ...
WELL? WHAT DO YOU THINK? IS IT ENOUGH PROOF?
I DON'T KNOW... WE'LL SEE...
WHAT IF WE PROVE IT'S GENUINE, THAT IT REALLY DATES FROM THE FIRST CENTURY?
WE'LL SEE...
43

PARIS...

MARCH 1314...

TWENTY-THREE YEARS AFTER THE SHIPWRECK OF THE FALCON TEMPLE...

SEVEN MONTHS AFTER THE ROCK SLIDE IN THE TUSCAN QUARRY...

OUR TEMPLE...

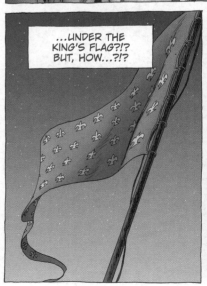

...UNDER THE KING'S FLAG?!? BUT, HOW...?!?

I SAY... THIS CASTLE ... ISN'T IT THE TEMPLE?

WHERE'VE YOU BEEN? YES ... IT USED TO BE!

44

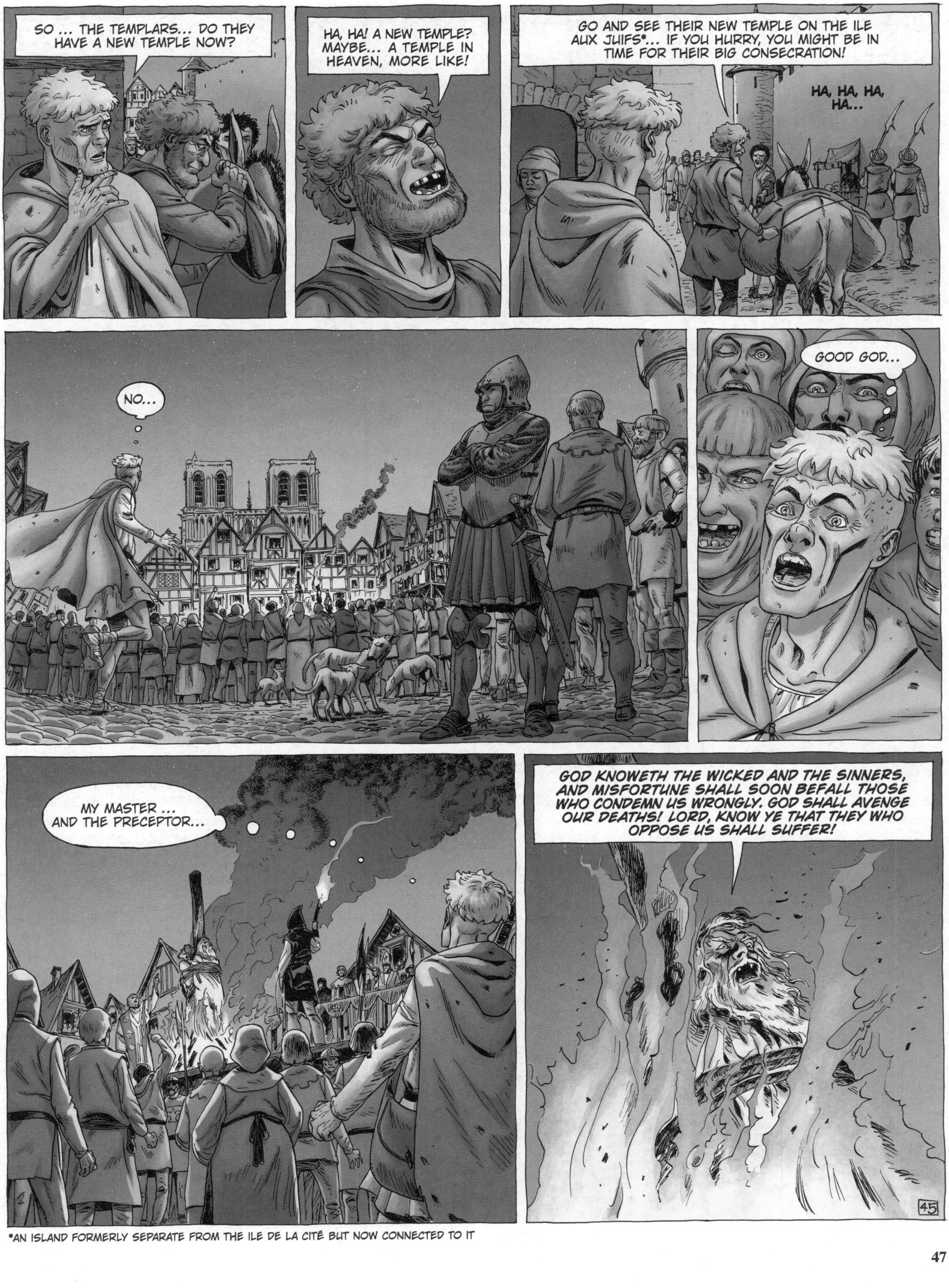
SO ... THE TEMPLARS... DO THEY HAVE A NEW TEMPLE NOW?
HA, HA! A NEW TEMPLE? MAYBE... A TEMPLE IN HEAVEN, MORE LIKE!
GO AND SEE THEIR NEW TEMPLE ON THE ILE AUX JUIFS*... IF YOU HURRY, YOU MIGHT BE IN TIME FOR THEIR BIG CONSECRATION!
HA, HA, HA, HA...
NO...
GOOD GOD...
MY MASTER ... AND THE PRECEPTOR...
GOD KNOWETH THE WICKED AND THE SINNERS, AND MISFORTUNE SHALL SOON BEFALL THOSE WHO CONDEMN US WRONGLY. GOD SHALL AVENGE OUR DEATHS! LORD, KNOW YE THAT THEY WHO OPPOSE US SHALL SUFFER!
45

*AN ISLAND FORMERLY SEPARATE FROM THE ILE DE LA CITÉ BUT NOW CONNECTED TO IT

BUT... THE RELIQUARY MASTER WILLIAM HANDED YOU IN ACRE... THE MANUSCRIPT IT CONTAINED...

THEY SEARCHED EVERYWHERE BENEATH THE TEMPLE ... BUT FOUND IT NOT...

THE GOSPEL OF JESUS?!?

IT'S A FORGERY. A FALSIFICATION THAT TOOK NINE YEARS OF PAINSTAKING LABOUR... BUT THEIR DECEPTION WAS SUCCESSFUL. THE VATICAN'S EXPERTS BELIEVED IT. IT WAS THE KEY TO OUR POWER ... AND IT'S STILL THE KEY TO OUR GRAND DESIGN, THIS PLAN THAT HAS TAKEN ALMOST TWO HUNDRED YEARS TO BEAR FRUIT ... AND WHICH MUST CONTINUE AT ANY PRICE.

YOU SEE, MARTIN? ALL THAT MATTERS IS THAT OUR ENEMIES THINK WE HAVE THE GOSPEL, AND BELIEVE IT TO BE GENUINE ... AND THAT THEY CARRY ON BELIEVING IT UNTIL WE FULFIL OUR ULTIMATE DESTINY...

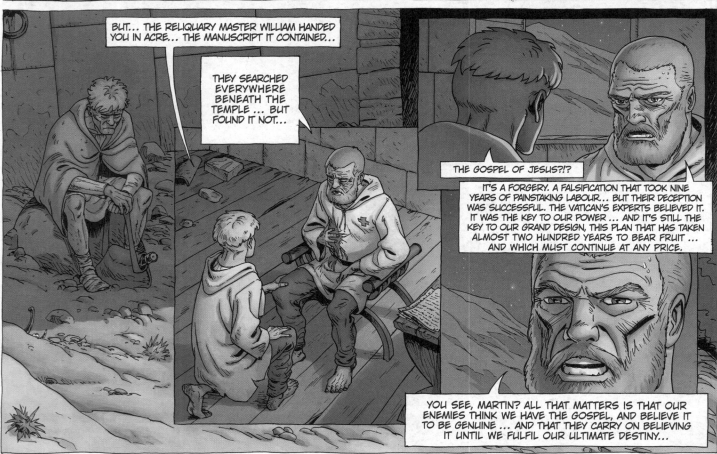

THAT DAY, AS I SET OFF FROM PARIS, I VOWED TO FIND THE MEANS TO MAKE SURE THE ILLUSION WAS KEPT ALIVE. IT HAD TO SURVIVE. SO THAT PEOPLE WOULD BELIEVE THE INCREDIBLE PROOF STILL EXISTED SOMEWHERE, BIDING ITS TIME.

AND AT THE RIGHT MOMENT, CERTAINLY NOT DURING MY LIFETIME, MAYBE SOMEONE WILL BE ABLE TO USE OUR LOST MASTERPIECE TO ACHIEVE WHAT WE HAD ALL SET OUT TO DO...

WHO KNOWS? MAYBE ONE DAY OUR GREAT PLAN WILL NO LONGER BE NECESSARY. MAYBE PEOPLE WILL HAVE LEARNED TO OVERCOME THEIR PETTY DIFFERENCES, TO STOP FIGHTING OVER MATTERS OF FAITH, AND TO RISE ABOVE ALL THESE RELIGIOUS SQUABBLES.

MAYBE...

THE END